PINDAR

POCKET

Print

Production

GUIDE

M. BARNARD, J. PEACOCK, C. BERRILL

BLUEPRINT

An Imprint of Chapman & Hall

London • Glasgow • Weinheim • New York • Tokyo • Melbourne • Madras

Published by Blueprint, an imprint of Chapman & Hall,
2–6 Boundary Row, London SE1 8HN, UK

Chapman & Hall, 2–6 Boundary Row, London SE1 8HN, UK

Blackie Academic & Professional, Wester Cleddens Road, Bishopbriggs, Glasgow G64 2NZ, UK

Chapman & Hall GmbH, Pappelallee 3, 69469 Weinheim, Germany

Chapman & Hall USA, 115 Fifth Avenue, New York, NY 10003, USA

Chapman & Hall Japan, ITP-Japan, Kyowa Building, 3F, 2-2-1 Hirakawacho, Chiyoda-ku, Tokyo 102, Japan

Chapman & Hall Australia, 102 Dodds Street, South Melbourne, Victoria 3205, Australia

Chapman & Hall India, R. Seshadri, 32 Second Main Road, CIT East, Madras 600 035, India

First edition 1995

© 1995 Blueprint

Printed in Great Britain at the University Press, Cambridge

ISBN 1 85713 005 7

A Catalogue record for this book is available from the British Library

The Pindar
Pocket Print Production Guide

Contents

Contents

Contents

Introduction

Some years ago we published a substantial reference manual for the printing and publishing industries: *The Print and Production Manual*. This has been reprinted through several editions and is serving a need, but it is necessarily a large and relatively expensive book which covers production subjects in a fairly comprehensive fashion. As with many large reference books, some of its content will be referred to occasionally rather than regularly.

The Pocket Production Guide is an attempt to distil the most regularly referenced material from the larger book into a smaller companion which is physically more manageable and can therefore be kept ready-to-hand.

Such a task is fraught with professional dangers for it is axiomatic that the least referred-to item of reference may be the most valuable in a given situation.

We therefore consulted many users of the *Manual* and potential users of the *Pocket Guide* and have tried to make selections based on their assessments as well as our own judgment. We hope the resulting content is useful. We would be interested in any suggestions for adjustment in later editions.

The editors would like to thank the many friends and colleagues from the trade associations and companies listed below who have helped with advice and information during the compilation of *The Pocket Prodution Guide:*

British Printing Industries Federation
British Paper and Board Industry Federation
British Standards Institution
Institute of Printing
Pira International
Publishers Association
Periodical Publishers Association
The Post Office
Turnergraphic Ltd
Monotype Systems Ltd
Linotype-Hell Ltd
Celloglass Ltd
Pindar plc

Specialist contributors:

Ian Faux
John Stephens
Geoffrey Winkley
Ron Strutt
Stuart Toberman
Geoff Todd
Technical staff of Robert Horne Ltd
Caryl Holland

1 Typography

Terms used

Although photocomposition has superseded hot-metal composition in all but a very few specialist applications, the industry is still some way from accepting or agreeing any new system of terms or typographical measurements which acknowledges this. Although BS Standard 4786:1972 offers an interesting recommendation for Metric Typographic Measurement, it seems unlikely ever to gain general commercial acceptance. The basis of type measurement and specification continues to be that derived from composition in metal, and most of the basic terms used have been carried through intact.

The basis: parts of a metal type character

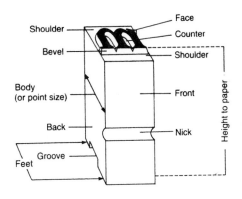

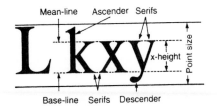

The printed image

1

Constitution of founts, families & series

Note the following definitions:

Fount

A complete set of *sorts*, all of the same typeface and point size, i.e. a complete set in one size and design of all the letters of the alphabet (upper case, small caps and lower case) with associated ligatures, numerals, punctuation marks and any other signs and symbols.

In a roman fount of type (say 11pt Times, for example) there are normally three alphabets: capitals, small capitals and lower case. In an italic or bold fount of type (say 11pt Times Italic or 11pt Times Bold, for example) there are normally two alphabets: capitals and lower case.

A roman (three alphabet) fount of type contains a range of sorts similar to:

Capitals: ABCDEFGHIJKLMNOPQRSTUVWXYZ
Small capitals: ABCDEFGHIJKLMNOPQRSTUVWXYZ
Lower case: abcdefghijklmnopqrstuvwxyz
Dipthongs: Æ, Œ, Æ, Œ, æ, œ
Ligatures: fi, fl, etc
Figures: 1,2,3,4,5,6,7,8,9,0
Punctuation marks: , ; . ? ! - – —
Reference marks: * (asterisk), † (dagger), ‡ (double dagger), § (section), ‖ (parallel)
Miscellaneous signs: () (parentheses), [] (brackets), & (ampersand)
Accented letters (or floating accents with which to make them):

á	é	í	ó	ú	(acute)
à	è	ì	ò	ù	(grave)
â	ê	î	ô	û	(circumflex)
ä	ë	ï		ö	ü	(diaresis)
ç (cedilla)		ñ (tilde)			

Fractions: $\frac{1}{4}, \frac{1}{2}, \frac{3}{4}, \frac{1}{8}, \frac{3}{8}, \frac{5}{8}, \frac{7}{8}, \frac{1}{3}, \frac{2}{3}, \frac{1}{6}$
Mathematical signs: = × ÷ + − ′ ″ °
Commercial signs: %, @, ©, ®, £, $, ¢

Family

A series of founts related to the basic text roman face.

Normally a type family will consist of a minimum of three founts - Roman, Italic, Bold - and

seven alphabets:
roman caps, roman small caps, roman lower case
italic caps, italic lower case
bold caps, bold lower case.

Many type families are considerably wider than these three basic fount designs, with versions in condensed, expanded, light, extra-light, extra-bold, etc. See the note on design variants below.

Series

A complete range of sizes in the same typeface, i.e. Baskerville 8pt, Baskerville 9pt, Baskerville 10pt, etc, is the Baskerville (roman) series.

Weight

The relative weights of a type family traditionally progress as follows:

Ultra-light
Extra-light
Light
Semi-light
MEDIUM
Semi-bold
Bold
Extra-bold
Ultra-bold.

Medium or *nominal* represents the design in its normal weight from which the variants are derived.

Width

The relative widths of a type family traditionally progress as follows:

Ultra-condensed
Extra-condensed
Condensed
Semi-condensed
MEDIUM
Semi-expanded
Expanded
Extra-expanded
Ultra-expanded.

Medium or nominal represents the basic design.

Design variants ('Designations')

Note that with the explosion of digital typesetting in the early 1970s, there was a tendency for some manufacturers to introduce their own versions of a typeface. Consequently, there can be variations in appearance between different manufacturers' versions of the same nominal typeface.

The same is true of the x-heights which may appear larger or smaller than might be expected from the nominal point size. Thus Agfa's 10 pt Garamond appears much smaller than Monotype's 10 pt Garamond, and both appear much smaller than 10 pt Helvetica.

Also note that the more versatile modern photosetting systems are capable of being programmed to create electronically almost infinite shades of variation to the basic design shape of a character, be it slant, weight or width. Desktop publishing systems can also create unusual variants. Detailed knowledge of the particular system being used is necessary when specifying such variants.

Variants

Variants

Variants

<u>Variants</u>

Variants

Variants

Variants

1

System of measurement

All printing measurements derive from the *point*, originally an imprecise unit of measurement used in the early days of printing for describing the body size of the founts of metal type in general use. Founts were described as 6-point type, 10-point type, etc., with each size having in addition its own name: 6-point was nonpareil, 10-point was long primer, etc., and the commonly-used 12-point size was called pica.

Originally an approximate measurement, the pica, survived as 12pts when it was standardized at .166044" in the 1870s in America, and became the accepted - and exact - unit of measurement for all typographical purposes in America and Great Britain.

A European system - originally from France - had earlier taken a slightly different measurement for the point as its standard (*didot* point), and hence for its 12pt pica (*cicero*). The European measures are some 7% larger than the Anglo-American measures.

Both systems are in use.

The important measurements to remember for quick calculation purposes (Anglo-American) are:

Point size	Inches	Millimetres
1pt	.014"	0.35mm
12pts	.166"	4.2mm

These figures are derived from the original exact measurements of 1 Anglo American pt = .013837", 1 pica = .166044"; 1 Didot pt = .0148", 1 cicero = .1776". The conversion factor from inches to millimetres is 25.400. The conversion factor from Anglo-American to Didot is 1.069596. The conversion factor from Didot to Anglo-American is 0.9349324.

The following pages show you a range of common 'text' faces up to 14-point and display faces up to 72-point.

All printing measurements derive from the *point*, originally an imprecise unit of measurement used in the early days of printing for describing the body size of the founts of metal type in general use.

6-point

All printing measurements derive from the *point*, originally an imprecise unit of measurement used in the early days of printing for describing the body size of the founts of metal type in general use.

8-point

All printing measurements derive from the *point*, originally an imprecise unit of measurement used in the early days of printing for describing the body size of the founts of metal type in general use.

9-point

All printing measurements derive from the *point*, originally an imprecise unit of measurement used in the early days of printing for describing the body size of the founts of metal type in general use.

10-point

All printing measurements derive from the *point*, originally an imprecise unit of measurement used in the early days of printing for describing the body size of the founts of metal type in general use.

11-point

All printing measurements derive from the *point*, originally an imprecise unit of measurement used in the early days of printing for describing the body size of the founts of metal type in general use.

12-point

All printing measurements derive from the *point*, originally an imprecise unit of measurement used in the early days of printing for describing the body size.

14-point

18-point Examples of sizes

24-point Examples of sizes

30-point Examples of

36-point Examples

48-point Exam

60-point Exam

72-point Exam

Space between lines of metal type was often increased by inserting strips of lead. This additional inter-line spacing is therefore known as *leading* and is also expressed in points . . . often in the form '10 on 11-point' or '12 on 14-point', meaning 10pt type with an additional 1pt between lines or 12pt type with an additional 2pts between lines.

Type set with no additional space between lines is said to be set *solid*.

Leading

Space between lines of metal type was often increased by inserting strips of lead. This additional inter-line spacing is therefore known as *leading* and is also expressed in points . . . often in the form '10 on 11-point' or '12 on 14-point', meaning 10pt type with an additional 1pt between lines or 12pt type with an additional 2pts between lines.

This example is 10pt solid.

Space between lines of metal type was often increased by inserting strips of lead. This additional inter-line spacing is therefore known as *leading* and is also expressed in points . . . often in the form '10 on 11-point' or '12 on 14-point', meaning 10pt type with an additional 1pt between lines or 12pt type with an additional 2pts between lines.

This is 10/11pt.

Space between lines of metal type was often increased by inserting strips of lead. This additional inter-line spacing is therefore known as *leading* and is also expressed in points . . . often in the form '10 on 11-point' or '12 on 14-point', meaning 10pt type with an additional 1pt between lines or 12pt type with an additional 2pts between lines.

While this is 10/14pt.

how to tell one face from another

Typeface design

Note these main features of type design which will help you distinguish one face from another:

Proportions

X-height and ascenders/descenders: note the relative sizes and relative weights. Character fit: note whether wide and loose fitting or compact and tight.

Stress

General angle of shading might be oblique (diagonal) or vertical. Note the degree of contrast between thick and thin strokes.

Serif formation

Can be bracketed or unbracketed. Can be oblique or horizontal in direction. Can be slab or hairline in weight.

British Standard 2961 was drawn up in 1967 and presents nine classifications. The 'traditional' nomenclature in operation before BS2961 is still in use, however, and is annotated alongside the British Standard classification where the two coincide. See also examples of alphabets in the *Typeface recognition* section.

Humanist

Traditionally known as 'Venetian' typefaces.

☐ light in weight, oblique stress, calligraphic in origin

- ☐ bar of lower-case 'e' inclined as in script handwriting
- ☐ bracketed serifs.

Examples: Centaur, Cloister Old Style, Horley Old Style, Kennerley, Veronese.

Garalde

Traditionally known as 'Old Face' or 'Old Style'.

- ☐ less calligraphic in appearance than Humanist styles
- ☐ oblique stress, but with horizontal 'e' bar.

Examples: Bembo, Caslon, Erhardt, Garamond, Imprint, Old Style, Plantin.

Transitional

Typefaces based on Baskerville's types of mid-18th century in Britain.

- ☐ axis of curves now vertical in stress. Rather more mechanical in appearance
- ☐ bracketed oblique serifs (as Garalde).

Examples: Baskerville, Bell, Caledonia, Fournier.

Didone

Traditionally known as 'Modern' typefaces.

- ☐ abrupt contrast between thick and thin strokes
- ☐ axis of curves completely vertical in stress
- ☐ horizontal top serifs, sometimes unbracketed hair-line.

Examples: Bodoni, Corvinus, Modern Extended, Walbaum.

Slab-serif

Otherwise called 'Egyptian'.

- ☐ Typefaces with heavy, square-ended serifs, with or without brackets.

Examples: Cairo, Clarendon, Egyptian, Playbill, Rockwell.

Lineale

- ☐ Typefaces without serifs, otherwise known as 'sans-serif'.

Four distinctions are made:

Grotesque

Lineales with 19th century origins. More 'closed' in appearance.
Examples: Grot 215, Headline Bold, Sans No. 7.

Neo-Grotesque

A later development, more rounded and open in design and monoline in weight.
Examples: Helvetica, Univers.

Geometric

Lineales constructed on simple geometric shapes, e.g. circle or rectangle.
Examples: Erbar, Eurostile, Futura.

Humanist

Based on the proportions of Humanist or Garalde lower-case, with stroke contrast.
Examples: Gill Sans, Optima, Pascal.

Glyphic

Typefaces based on a chiselled rather than a calligraphic form.
☐ Blunt, elephant-foot serifs.
Examples: Albertus, Chisel, Festival, Latin.

Script

Typefaces that imitate cursive writing.
Two distinctions are made:

Formal

Examples: Marina, Palace Script.

Informal

Examples: Flash, Mistral, Pepita.

Graphic

Typefaces which appear to have been drawn graphically rather than written.

Examples: Cartoon, Klang, Libra, Old English.

Note: The traditional category of '20th century' bookfaces which are mainly hybrid in origin are defined under BS2961 by reference to their double origin, e.g.:

☐ Juliana - Humanist - Garalde

☐ Times New Roman - Garalde-Didone.

Examples of such hybrids include: Goudy Old Style, Lectura, Melior, Photina, Pilgrim, Spectrum.

2 Copy preparation

Presentation from the author (hard copy)

Where you can influence this, advise the following:

☐ manuscript to be wordprocessed or typewritten, double-spaced and on one side of the sheet only

☐ all folios the same size (A4 preferably)

☐ an equal number of lines per folio, with no extra space between paragraphs

☐ lines printed out or typed to approximately the same length, with two spaces paragraph indent only; ample left-hand margin

☐ handwritten corrections to follow standard proof correction symbols given later in this section

☐ any headings or sub-headings in the text to be indicated in level of importance as A, B, C, etc.

☐ extracts or footnotes in long manuscripts to be typed in with the main text, colour-coded for quick identification and placed immediately below their reference with a line space and dividing line above and below them.

Check through for the following and amend if necessary:

☐ all folios numbered in sequence, with any subsequently deleted folios struck through but left in the manuscript

☐ no pins or staples

☐ any additional matter typed on separate folios of the same size as the rest of the manuscript and marked A (109A, 123A, etc.). Mark at the head of additional copy TAKE IN FROM INSERTION MARK ON FOLIO. . . (previous main folio) and at the foot of additional copy

Text preparation

Manuscript assembly for magazine or bookwork

RETURN TO INSERTION MARK ON FOLIO
... (the same previous main folio). At the same
time, mark the main folio affected with an insertion indication CONTINUE WITH FOLIO
109A, 123A, etc. THEN RETURN

☐ in magazine work, be sure to write clearly
which sections ('departments') of the magazine
the manuscript copy in hand has been prepared
for, e.g. NEWS, BACKGROUND, LETTERS
PAGES.

☐ in bookwork, assemble the manuscript in the
following divisions: prelims (with breakdown),
main text (with breakdown), endmatter (with
breakdown). Later in this section there is a
detailed note on the conventional order of contents within each of these divisions.

Illustration assembly

Check the following:

☐ all photographs and colour artwork to be
kept separate from the text manuscript but keyed
for position by cross-reference with the manuscript
☐ all line illustrations treated separately, and
as separate batches apart from half-tones
☐ captions to illustrations sent all together as a
batch of copy.

Be sure to advise on any originals which are damaged or of such poor quality that they might be
unacceptable when printed. More detailed notes on
dealing with illustrations appear later in this section
and in the *Origination* section.

Camera-ready copy

With the advent of electronic typewriters and word
processors it became acceptable practice with some
forms of publishing to use the author's typed manuscript as camera-ready artwork, reducing/enlarging
it if necessary to fit the final page.

Whether this is aesthetically acceptable is a
decision to be made by the publisher and his sales
department. Whether it is a practical method of
operation depends partly on the likely level of
correction to the original manuscript, partly on the
facilities for and keenness about re-typing the de-
faced artwork after editing.

It must be agreed between author and publisher at the outset what processes of editing and correction will take place and who will perform them.

If it is accepted that the original manuscript is simply a draft and that there will be a completely re-typed final version, then it matters not how the original is presented, within the normal standards of presenting copy for editing. The final typed version, however, will need to conform to style in a number of important respects.

House style will need to be agreed in detail. A proper style book should be prepared and must be followed by the author and editor scrupulously. It may be possible to make corrections fairly simply on a word processor or dtp system, but it will be very irritating to re-type a complete page on a typewriter because an abbreviation has been handled incorrectly.

As with keying electronic manuscripts, there will need to be consistent rules for spacing around punctuation and these may not be what the typist learnt at secretarial college. Additionally the presentational style for headings, footnotes, lists, tables, emphasized text of one sort or another, and so on, will need agreeing, specifying and possibly modifying to suit the facilities which exist on the author's own machine.

The editor will need to specify what must happen when characters are needed which cannot be generated on the typewriter or computer - hand-drawn, Letraset, etc. - and must not forget in this respect the problematic use of hyphens and dashes . . . not the same character on the printed page. For reference, here is a hyphen, an en dash and an em dash:

Preparing camera copy

For strike-on composition a carbon ribbon should be used to give a clear, crisp impression.

With founts which are larger than normal typesetting text sizes, some degree of reduction of the original may be necessary.

Proportionately spaced letters and words look more pleasing.

If electronic printing is to be used it should be at least 'near-letter quality'. Some 'special sorts' - especially chemical and mathematical symbols - may not be available on the output system used and some means of creating these must be considered.

Sub-editing, mark-up
and design

To avoid misunderstandings, these areas of responsibility should be recognized, defined and allotted to either publisher or typesetter.

Areas of responsibility

For sub-editorial work (almost always accepted as the responsibility of the publisher):

☐ factual accuracy of the text
☐ avoidance of potential libel problems or copyright problems in the text
☐ application of an agreed sub-editorial style or house style (as below) as appropriate
☐ instruction to the typographic/design team
☐ identification of grades of heading, emphases, etc.
☐ notification of special sorts, etc.

For typographical design:

☐ visual appearance of the work: type area, typefaces to be used, treatment of parts of the work, section or chapter heads, extracts, etc.

For keyboard mark-up of hard copy (normally the typesetter's responsibility):

☐ technical, keyboarding or coding instructions specific to the machine in use
☐ typographical instructions furthering in detail the main specification already given by the typographical/design team.

House style for magazine or bookwork

Many companies follow one of the standard works of reference rather than having an individual house style:

☐ Hart, *Hart's Rules for Compositors and Readers at the University Press, Oxford*
☐ Butcher, *Copy-editing. The Cambridge Handbook*
☐ Collins, *Author's and Printers' Dictionary.*

2

Traditionally, typesetting companies invariably 'followed copy' so the application of style to a manuscript in detail was firmly the publisher's responsibility. However, today typesetters are normally prepared to take on this role if instructed as well as query any anomalies that they come across.

Common points of detail which go to make up a house style include decisions on:

☐ alternative spellings
-ise or -ize, enquire/inquire, acknowledgement/acknowledgment, etc. (reference books carry lists)

☐ punctuation rules
use of full point after abbreviations and after titles (the trend is towards mimimum use)
double or single quotation marks in speech (single quotation marks look less obtrusive)
en rule or em dash (one en is more common)
use of reference marks or superior figures (correct order of reference marks is *, †, ‡, §,‖, ¶

☐ use of italic or quotes for titles, etc.

☐ use of hyphens and word divisions
number of successive word breaks permissible at line-endings (two is normal)
whether a hyphen can separate a word between pages (normally no)
any house preferences in optional word divisions

☐ use of figures
when to use lining figs and when non-lining (might depend on typeface)
when numbers are written out (normally under 10)

☐ typographical and page make-up points
whether the following are allowed:
club line - the first line of a new paragraph at the foot of a page
widow - one word (end of paragraph) on its own at the head of a page
widow line - short line (less than half measure) on its own at the head of a page
breakword - a word broken between the foot of one page and the head of the next.

2

Typographical considerations

These are some of the conventions commonly applied, particularly for bookwork. Magazine design tends to vary considerably although the basic rules still apply.

Prelims

Best paginated separately from the main text, if extensive, in order to allow pagination of main text independently and without risk of change if prelims are modified.

An accepted order of prelims in bookwork is:

☐ half-title page - traditional opening page (to protect title page)

☐ advertisement* - often 'by the same author', etc.

☐ title page - title, author, publisher

☐ copyright page* - also called 'history page' or 'biblio page'. Details of edition record, copyright notice and printer's imprint

☐ dedication - either here or, alternatively, on left-hand page facing first page of text

☐ acknowledgements* - list of sources, references, etc

☐ contents list - list of chapters

☐ list of illustrations

☐ list of abbreviations - mainly in dictionaries, encyclopaedias, etc.

☐ foreword - written by a person other than the author

☐ preface - written by the author himself (personal remarks about book)

☐ introduction - normally written by the author himself (concerning subject-matter).

*This material normally occupies a left-hand page. All other items commence on a right-hand page wherever possible.

Main text

Consideration needs to be given to the treatment of:

☐ body text setting and subsidiary text setting

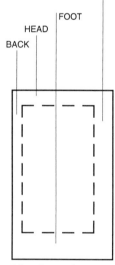

Margins and conventional ratios.

FORE-EDGE

FOOT

HEAD

BACK

☐ display heads and subheads
☐ headlines and folios.

Body text setting and subsidiary text setting

The following suggestions represent merely conventional wisdom. An infinite number of variants is possible.

Choice of typeface. A question of the availability at the supplier and of the designer's taste. The most commonly used bookwork faces are such serif faces as Baskerville, Bembo, Century, Garamond, Plantin, Times. Sans-serif faces - Helvetica, Univers, etc. - are harder to read in continuous text than serif faces and are generally not advisable for long stretches of type.

Note that there can be wide variations in appearance between different manufacturers' versions of the same nominal typeface and it is always prudent to see specimens of a face in the chosen system before specifying.

Choice of size. It is important to check appearing sizes as well as specifying point size. Firstly, manufacturers' designs of the same face differ widely and secondly typefaces with particularly large or small x-heights may appear larger or smaller than you might expect from nominal point size. Thus, Agfa's 10pt Garamond, for example, is much smaller in appearing size than Monotype's 10pt Garamond, and 10pt Garamond in either system is much smaller in appearing size than 10pt Helvetica. Even more extreme examples may occur.

Choice of margins and type area. A suitable type measure for a conventional printed book page is about three-quarters of the width of the page, the remaining quarter being divided in the conventional proportions of 1:2, the back or inside margin being the smaller and the fore-edge or outer margin the greater.

A conventional proportion of margins is 1/1.5/2/ 2.5 for back:head:fore-edge:foot . . . or near to this.

In stipulating the position of a type area on a page, it is conventional to specify the back margin and the head margin exactly and to let the fore-edge margin and the foot margin form themselves.

In specifying a type area, be sure to make clear

Text setting conventions

When specifying continuous text setting, you might find the following conventions useful to bear in mind:

1. Do not set a type size to a measure more than half its point size in inches, e.g. do not set 10pt (or 10/11pt or 10/1, etc.) to more than 5" (30 picas).

2. When specifying leading, aim for a result that gives 1 - 1.5 x-heights of white space between lines when viewed. In practice, this will normally mean 1pt or 2pts leaded in sizes up to 12pt; 3pts or 4pts leaded in sizes 14 - 18pt. Sizes above this will normally be display headings.

Extracts are conventionally set two sizes down, with half-line or one line space above and below.

Tables are conventionally set two sizes down, with half-line or one line space above and below.

whether you mean the inclusive type area, i.e. inclusive of running headline, white line and foot folio, as well as the main text itself, or the exclusive type area, which consists only of the main text without allowance for headlines or folios.

The following inclusive type areas and margins for the standard metric octavo book sizes work acceptably.

Trimmed page	mm size	Type area (picas)	Back (picas)	Head (picas)	Fore-edge (picas)	Foot (picas)
Small format paperback	178x111	35x21	2	2½	3½	5
Crown 8vo	186x123	36x22	2½	2½	4½	5½
Large Crown 8vo	198x129	38x23	3	3	4½	5½
Demy 8vo	216x138	42x24	3½	3½	5	5½
Royal 8vo	234x156	45x28	4	4	5	6½

Typical sizes which could be added to this for a complete specification are as follows:

Trimmed page	mm size	Typical specifications					
		type size (pts)	lines per page inc/exc headline	ens per line	words per line	ens of setting per page	actual words per page
Small format paperback	178x111	9/10	42/40	61½	11	2325	425
Crown 8vo	186x123	10/11	39/37	58	10½	2050	375
Large Crown 8vo	198x129	10/11	41/39	61	10½	2275	400
Demy 8vo	216x138	11/12	42/40	58½	10½	2200	400
Royal 8vo	234x156	11/13	41/39	67	12	2475	450

Quarto and larger paper sizes are the normal formats for illustrated publications, often with double- or treble-column settings, and so typical type areas are harder to suggest in the same degree of detail. The following inclusive type areas may be acceptable for conventionally laid-out material:

Trimmed page	mm size	Type area (picas)	Back (picas)	Head (picas)	Fore-edge (picas)	Foot (picas)
Crown 4to	246x189	50x37	3½	3	4½	5½
Demy 4to	276x219	58x44	3½	3	4½	4½
A4	297x210	62x42	3½	4	4½	5

Typical type sizes may be 11/12pt for double-column settings or 10/11pt for treble-column settings, with typical word counts per page being:

Trimmed page	mm size	11/12pt double-column	10/11pt treble-column
Crown 4to	246x189	700	850
Demy 4to	276x219	800	975
A4	297x210	900	1100

Display heads and subheads

Display heads and subheads are normally dropped from the head of the page (specified in lines or picas off the exclusive type area). They can be ranged left or right or centred in such a way as headlines, and it is common practice to let headline and heading positionings echo each other.

Subheads are conventionally set as either:

☐ boxed - ranged left to measure
☐ cross - centred over the measure.

Boxed heads can be either:

☐ side heads - frequently text caps or italics, with text running on in same line
☐ shoulder heads - occupy a line alone with text commencing flush below or indented.

Shoulder heads are frequently used to break up text into subsections. They are often set text bold, and balance well with about three times as much space above as below (say 9pts space above and 3pts space below for 11/12pt main text setting).

Cross-heads are usually centred over the measure. You would normally expect to use a cross-head for greater emphasis than a boxed head.

The conventional levels of importance in headings, in ascending order, are:

☐ side head *and, or*
☐ shoulder head *and, or*
☐ cross-head
☐ display heading (chapter or part, etc.).

Headlines and folios

A running head, strictly, is a headline which is repeated unchanged throughout, normally the main title of the book or the title and date of the magazine. Conventional arrangements in bookwork are:

☐ fiction
VERSO - book title (invariable)
RECTO - chapter title or section title (variable)
☐ non-fiction
VERSO - chapter title or section title (variable)

RECTO - subsection title (variable)

Conventional positions might be:

☐ ranged to fore-edge margin or indented 1/2/3/4 picas in, italics or roman
☐ centred, italics or roman
☐ ranged to back margin or indented 1/2/3/4 picas in, italics or roman.

Note that less than one line space below is frequently sufficient to show separation from main text. Likewise small caps (letterspaced) may often be visually preferable to text-sized caps.

Folios are conventionally either ranged with the headline at the head of the page (centred r/l, r/r), or at the foot of the page with half a line or one line separation from the text. Text size is normally suitable.

Endmatter

Traditionally, endmatter items in bookwork are placed in this order:

☐ appendix/appendices - tables, plans, etc. relating to the text, but not directly part of it
☐ notes - explanatory notes
☐ glossary - explanation of terms used
☐ vocabulary - in conjunction with, or instead of, a glossary in (say) foreign language textbooks
☐ bibliography - list of reference sources
☐ index - alphabetical indicator of subjects.

All these items normally commence on a right-hand page.

Appendices and notes are normally one size smaller than body text. Glossaries, vocabularies, bibliographies and indices are frequently two sizes smaller than body text.

Illustrations

Full procedures for the scaling of originals are described in the section on *Origination*.

The basic steps are:

☐ 1. Determine the general proportions desired in the printed result (square, rectangle etc.).

Then, bearing in mind these general proportions, determine the approximate area of the original that you want to display. Mask out the areas of the original that you know from the outset you have to delete.

☐ 2. Ascertain the exact size of one dimension at which you need the printed illustration to appear. If working to a grid, for example, this might be the width of a one-column measure in a magazine; or the type measure in a book; or a predetermined width of box in a sequence of boxed illustrations.

☐ 3. Returning to the original, examine this same dimension (say the width) and measure the width of original which represents the contents you want to appear in the printed result. Mark this width (as two vertical lines) either on an overlay over the original or on the back of the original.

☐ 4. If the dimension in para 2 is xmm and the dimension in para 3 is ymm, then x divided by y is the reduction factor being proposed (it might be 80% or 90%, etc.). Note this.

☐ 5. Look now at the depth of illustration required in the finished result. If the depth of the printed result is already determined by the requirement of layout, follow step 5a. If the depth of the printed result is flexible, follow step 5b.

a. Say the reduction in (4) is 80%. Then the depth of the original which you are allowed in order to arrive at your finished version will be 100 divided by 80 multiplied by your fixed depth of finished version. Calculate what this is, and mask off the original in its depth accordingly. If this masking would delete an important part of the picture, you must either compromise and change this 'fixed' depth, adjusting other elements of the layout accordingly, or start again at para 3 with a different definition of the width dimension by masking more or less than you did before. This will achieve a different reduction factor and with trial and error will lead you to an acceptable result in the depth allowance of the original.

b. Say the reduction in (4) is 80%. Then turn to

the original, choose your ideal depth of subject and mask this off. Then this depth of original x 80% gives the depth of the finished picture which will result.

Conventional bookwork instructions – summary example

The following is a typical set of conventional instructions for straightforward bookwork setting and page make-up which you may find useful for reference.

Spacing parameters

☐ Letterspacing within lines not allowed.
☐ Vertical justification ('feathering') not allowed.
☐ Wordspacing: average 12-15 units; min 9 units; max 39 units (based on 54 unit em; use equivalent values for different systems as relevant).

Page layout

☐ Page depths to be equal across each spread; if unavoidable, spreads may be left one line long or short to achieve this, but facing pages must always be equal.
☐ At least four lines of text should appear on the final page of each chapter; previous verso on spread may be left short to achieve this.
☐ Avoid widows at tops of pages; if absolutely unavoidable, a limited number per book is acceptable provided that the line is at least half full. At no time are two widows across a spread acceptable.
☐ If a run-on chapter or section within a chapter falls near the foot of a page at least two lines must appear at foot of page. It is not acceptable for the last line of a section/displayed extract to appear at the top of a page.
☐ If line spaces marked in copy fall at top/foot of a page, insert asterisk, centred on measure, at foot of previous page.

H&J/wordbreaks

☐ For general rules, follow *Hart's Rules*. For guidance on breaking specific words follow

Collins' Gem Dictionary of Spelling and Word Division.

☐ No more than two successive lines to end with hyphens; no further hyphens allowed within two lines.

☐ Hyphens not allowed in last word of a page.

☐ Compound words must always be broken at the existing hyphen, i.e. no second hyphen to be introduced.

☐ Try to avoid splitting dates, initials and names wherever possible.

☐ Unacceptable wordbreaks will be marked on proof for typesetter to correct (i.e. proofreader will not try to indicate solution). Any consequent new hyphenation to be typesetter's responsibility.

Folios and running heads

☐ Prelims: number in roman; arabic folios begin with first page of main text unless otherwise indicated on individual typescript.

☐ Running heads: in main text, set book title on versos, chapter title on rectos, unless otherwise instructed; in frontmatter/endmatter set section title (e.g. Preface, Index) on rectos and versos.

☐ Folios: no folio on part title or verso, or on opening page of chapter. Always set folio on chapter ends and final page of book.

☐ Paragraphs: set first line of opening paragraph or section within a chapter full out. Indent first lines of subsequent paragraphs one em of set.

Miscellaneous textual notes

☐ Use single quotes and double within single unless otherwise instructed. In quote-within-quote use hair-space between double and single quote marks.

☐ 'Parenthetical' en-dashes to be word-spaced.

☐ Em dashes may be set either closed-up to previous word or word-spaced, according to context: follow copy.

☐ Full points, commas, colons, semi-colons, etc. to be set closed-up to preceding word, followed by word space.

☐ Ellipses: three dot or four, according to context. If three, space dots with fixed thin spaces. If four, full-point closed up to preceding word, followed by thin space and three dot ellipses as above.

☐ No more than two successive lines of text to begin or end with the same word.

☐ Phrases or groups of words which appear in successive lines must not be set in the same position in both lines.

Much of the above may be set out on a composition order form.

Printing considerations

There are a number of considerations which affect how the job is printed, but which need to be taken into account at the design and copy preparation stage.

Typefaces with delicate hairline serifs (e.g. Bodini) are more demanding to reproduce than more robust, consistently thicker faces (e.g. Univers).

Where text matter is to be printed in more than one of the process colours, or is to be reversed out of a panel made up of process colour tints or a four colour halftone, be sure that the type size is sensibly large, and that the serifs are not too fine. Any delicate typeface reversed out from a number of colours will risk being spoiled. Choose the minimum number of colours possible in reversing out to white for a coloured panel.

Where type or line is being printed in a special colour outside the process range, use a generally accepted colour code to inform the printer (e.g. a Pantone reference number) and attach a swatch to the artwork as an additional aid.

Go for the best quality paper possible within the budget available. A poor paper surface will put a very definite upper limit on the quality of halftone possible, regardless of the quality of the original.

When assessing the maximum area of the printed image, it needs to be remembered that an allowance needs to be made for the press's grippers. The

2

actual amount can vary and needs to be checked with the printer.

So as to achieve the most economical method of positioning the pages for use of colour, it is customary to make up a flat-plan of page positions. This not only shows where four, two or single colours may fall, but also allows the balance of content to be assessed. (See page 146 for more details.)

Proof reading and correction

Proofs from phototypeset material, in either galley or page form, can be produced by one of the following methods:

☐ photocopying (if from bromides or hard copy)
☐ blueprinting or diazo copying (if from film)
☐ electronic printer

Bear in mind that either of the first two methods may not be able to give top quality reproduction of the typematter image, and incidental spots or distortions are best checked against original CRC/film if it is available before being automatically marked for attention in the proof. Although photocopying has improved significantly in recent years, bear in mind, too, that when photocopied galleys are being used (for example in rough paste-ups for position), enlargements of 102-103% are possible with some photocopiers. This means that a rough paste-up on a grid drawn for columns of 60 lines 8/9pt (540pts) will need to overhang by some 10-15pts at the foot - or apparently some 1.5-2 lines of text - in order to compensate for this level of distortion.

Where modern phototypesetting equipment is being used, it is common for first proofs to be produced not by the typesetter itself on to film or bromide paper but by a digital printer on to plain paper. The proof quality will depend on the equipment being used, the laser printing having now mainly replaced line, daisywheel and dot matrix machines. The resulting quality should be better than producing proofs from bromides, since it is first rather than a second generation copy.

Standard proof correction marks

British Standard BS 5261:Part 2 1976 specifies a comprehensive system of proof correction marks which does not rely on the use of English words or letters, and which is officially endorsed by the Publishers Association and the British Printing Industries Federation. For obvious reasons it is particularly useful when dealing with proof corrections internationally. It is detailed in the following pages.

Marks are best made in ink, using the following colour scheme:

☐ red: indicating errors introduced by the type-setter and to be corrected at his expense

☐ blue: indicating author's alterations (AA) required, which may be charged extra

☐ green: comments/corrections noted by the typesetter's reader, and marked on the proofs before they are sent out.

Note that corrections to photoset matter are nor-mally carried out in one of two ways:

☐ the operator sets line or patch corrections, which are then pasted or stripped in by hand on the CRC/film by a make-up artist

☐ the operator recalls the text from the compu-ter file on a visual display unit, makes the correc-tion required on the screen, and regenerates a new page/part of a page.

The second method is to be preferred to the first since densities can vary with patch corrections and the electronic file may remain uncorrected.

The most common proof correction marks are shown on the following pages.

INSTRUCTION	TEXTUAL MARK	MARGINAL MARK
Correction is concluded	None	/
Leave unchanged	— — — — — — — under characters to remain	✓
Remove extraneous marks	Encircle marks to be removed	✕
Push down risen spacing material	Encircle blemish	⊥
Refer to appropriate authority anything of doubtful accuracy	Encircle words affected	?
Insert in text the matter indicated in the margin	⋏	New matter followed by: ⋏
Insert additional matter identified by a letter in a diamond	⋏	⋏ Followed by, for example: ◇A
Delete	/ through character(s) or ⊢———⊣ though words to be deleted	♂
Delete and close up	/ through character or ⊢———⊣ through characters eg chara͜cter chara͜cter	♂
Substitute character or substitute part of one or more word(s)	/ through character or ⊢———⊣ through word(s)	New character or new word(s)

INSTRUCTION	TEXTUAL MARK	MARGINAL MARK
Wrong fount. Replace by character(s) or correct fount	Encircle characters to be changed	
Change damaged characters	Encircle character(s) to be changed	
Set in or change to italic	under character(s) to be set or changed	
Set in or change to capital letters	under character(s) to be set or changed	
Set in or change to small capital letters	under characters to be set or changed	
Set in or change to capital letters for initial letters and small capital letters for the rest of the words	under initial letters and under the rest of the word(s)	
Set in or change to bold type	under character(s) to be set or changed	
Set in or change to bold italic type	under character(s) to be set or changed	
Change capital letters to lower case letters	Encircle character(s) to be changed	
Change small capital letters to lower case letters	Encircle character(s) to be changed	
Change italic to upright type	Encircle character(s) to be changed	

INSTRUCTION	TEXTUAL MARK	MARGINAL MARK
Invert type	Encircle character to be inverted	
Substitute or insert character in 'superior' position	through character or where required	under character eg
Substitute or insert character in 'inferior' position	through character or where required	over character eg
Substitute ligature eg fl for separate letters	through characters affected	eg fl
Substitute separate letters for ligature		Write out separate letters
Substitute or insert full stop or decimal point	through character or where required	
Substitute or insert colon	through character or where required	
Substitute or insert semi-colon	through character or where required	
Substitute or insert comma	through character or where required	

INSTRUCTION	TEXTUAL MARK	MARGINAL MARK
Substitute or insert apostrophe	/ through character or ⟍ where required	⟋
Substitute or insert single quotation marks	/ through character or ⟍ where required	⟋ and/or ⟋
Substitute or insert double quotation marks	/ through character or ⟍ where required	⟋ and/or ⟋
Substitute or insert ellipsis	/ through character or ⟍ where required	. . .
Substitute or insert leader dots	/ through character or ⟍ where required	(⋯)
Substitute or insert hyphen	/ through character or ⟍ where required	⊢─⊣
Substitute or insert rule	/ through character or ⟍ where required	⊢─⊣
Substitute or insert oblique	/ through character or ⟍ where required	(⟋)
Start new paragraph	⌐_	⌐_
Run on (no new paragraph)	⌒⟩	⌒⟩

INSTRUCTION	TEXTUAL MARK	MARGINAL MARK
Transpose characters or words	between characters or words, numbered where necessary	
Transpose a number of characters or words	3 2 1	123
Transpose lines		
Transpose a number of lines	3 2 1	
Centre	Enclosing matter to be centred	[ ]
Indent		
Cancel indent		
Set line justified to specified measure	and/or	
Set column justified to specified measure		
Move matter specified distance to the right	enclosing matter to be moved to the right	
Move matter specified distance to the left	enclosing matter to be moved to the left	

INSTRUCTION	TEXTUAL MARK	MARGINAL MARK
Take over character(s), word(s) or line to next line, column or page		
Take back character(s), word(s) or line to previous line, column or page		
Raise matter	over matter to be raised under matter to be raised	
Lower matter	over matter to be lowered under matter to be lowered	
Move matter to position indicated	Enclose matter to be moved and indicate new position	
Correct vertical alignment		
Correct horizontal alignment	Single line above and below misaligned matter eg misaligned	
Close up. Delete space between characters or words	Delete space	
Insert space between characters	between characters affected	
Insert space between words	between words affected	

INSTRUCTION	TEXTUAL MARK	MARGINAL MARK
Make space appear equal between characters or words	between characters or words affected	
Close up normal interline spacing	(each side of column linking lines)	
Insert space between lines or paragraphs	or	
Reduce space between lines or paragraphs	or	
Reduce space between characters	between characters affected	
Reduce space between words	between words affected	

2

A further set of conventions applies in correcting mathematical or scientific typesetting. These are the common mathematical symbols and –opposite – their correction marks.

Mathematical symbols

(Parenthesis

[Bracket

{ Brace

⟨ Angle bracket or 'Bra'

⟩ Angle bracket, colloquially 'Ker'

⟦ Open bracket

! Factorial sign

· Decimal point

′ Prime

″ Double prime

‴ Triple prime

⁗ Quadruple prime

° Degree

∵ Because or since

∴ Therefore, hence

: Sign of proportion

:: Sign of proportion

≶ Less than or greater than

≷ Greater than or less than

≦ Less than or equal to

⩽ Less than or equal to

⪇ Not less than nor equal to

⪈ Not greater than nor equal to

/ Divided by, solidus

| Modulus used thus |x|

‖ Parallel to

≡ Congruent to

⧣ Equal or parallel

ↅ Between

∞ Infinity

∝ Varies as, proportional to

√ Radical sign

+ Plus

− Minus

× Multiply

÷ Divide

± Plus or minus

= Equal to

≠ Is not equal to

≈ Approximately equal to

⊻ Equiangular (geometry)

→ Approaches/tends to the limit

↔ Mutually implies

⊃ Implies

⊂ Is implied by

⊆ Contained as sub-set within

≑ Approximately equal to

≏ Approximately equal to

≃ Approximately equal to

∼ Difference between

≁ Is not asymptotic to

≈ Is approximately asymptotic to

< Less than

> Greater than

≮ Not less than

≯ Not greater than

≳ Equivalent to or greater than

≲ Equivalent to or less than

≪ Much less than

≫ Much greater than

⋘ Not much less than

⋙ Not much greater than

⊇ Contains as sub-set

∃ There exists

Γ Gamma function

∂ Partial differentiation

F Digamma function

∫ Integral

∮ Contour integral

Mathematical correction marks

Alteration required	Mark in margin	Mark in text
Use Greek letter	Letter required followed by (Gk)	/ Through letter
Use German (Fraktur) letter	Letter required followed by (Gar)	/ Through letter
Use roman	Letter required followed by (Rom)	/ Through letter
Use script	Letter required followed by (Scr)	/ Through letter
Use superior to superior (eg '2' in y^{a^2})	x — Showing letter required	/ Through letter
Use inferior to inferior (eg '2' in y_{a_2})	x — Showing letter required	/ Through letter
Use superior to inferior (eg '2' in y_{a^2})	x — letter required	/ Through letter
Use inferior to superior (eg '2' in y^{a_2})	x — Showing letter required	/ Through letter
Use figure	(fig) 1/2/etc	/ Through letter
Use fraction made up two lines deep	*2-line frac*	Circle around fraction
Use text size fraction	*10pt frac* (According to point size)	Circle around fraction
Use a decimal point	(dec)	∨/
Space to be hair space or 2 units or either a thick space or 5 units as indicated	*hair* (2#) *thick #* (5#)	∧ Where required

Foreign language setting

Foreign language setting invariably requires access to a range of accents or special characters. These are checklists of the more common ones.

Accents and special characters

Acute accent

e.g. é used in many foreign languages, notably French.

Cedilla

e.g. ç used in many languages, notably French where it alters the pronunciation of c.

Diaeresis

The same sign as the umlaut, used in English over the second of two vowels to show that they are to be sounded separately, e.g. Noël.

Diphthong

Vowel ligatures Æ Œ æ œ. These are used in Old English words e.g. Ælfric, Cædmon, and in French words such as manœuvre.

Eszett

ß, a character used in many German words when a double s occurs. Not used in caps or small caps.

Grave accent

e.g. è used in many foreign languages, notably French. (Also used in English poetry to indicate that an ordinarily mute syllable should be sounded separately.)

Tilde

eg ñ an accent used in Spanish and Portuguese.

Umlaut

e.g. ü used in foreign languages, notably German, to alter pronunciation of a, o, u (transliterated ae,oe,ue).

å ø

Used in Scandinavian languages, called by the sounds they represent: å as au in author and ø as o in word.

2

Accents of major European and Scandinavian languages

Albanian	â ç ë
Czech	á č ď é ě í ň ó ř š ť ú ů ý ž
Danish	å æ ø
Dutch	æ é è ê ë ó ò ô ij
Esperanto	ĉ ĝ ĵ ŝ ŭ (ĥ)
Finnish	ä å ö
Flemish	ë ó ij
French	à â ç é è ë î ï ô œ ù û ü
German	ä ö ü ß
Hungarian	á é í ó ö ő ú ü ű
Icelandic	á æ ð é í ó ö œ þ ú ý
Italian	à é è í ì î ó ò ù ú
Norwegian	å æ ø
Polish	ą ć ę ł ń ó ś ź ż
Portuguese	á à â ã ç é è ê í ì ó ò ô õ ú ù
Rumanian	à â ă è ì î ş ţ ù
Serbo-Croatian	č ć đ š ž
Spanish	á é í ñ ó ú ü
Swedish	å ä ö
Turkish	â ç ğ ı î ö ş ü û İ
Welsh	ä â ë ê ï î ö ô ŵ ÿ ŷ

Old English
special
characters

Þ þ   Thorn
Ð ð   Eth
Ʒ ʒ   Yogh

𝕬 𝖆	Aa	𝕺 𝖔	Oo
𝕬 ä	Ää	𝕺 ö	Öö
𝕭 𝖇	Bb	𝕻 𝖕	Pp
𝕮 𝖈	Cc	𝕼 𝖖	Qq
𝕯 𝖉	Dd	𝕽 𝖗	Rr
𝕰 𝖊	Ee	𝕾 𝖘	Ss
𝕱 𝖋	Ff	𝕿 𝖙	Tt
𝕲 𝖌	Gg	𝖀 𝖚	Uu
𝕳 𝖍	Hh	𝖀 ü	Üü
𝕴 i or i	Ii, Jj	𝖁 𝖛	Vv
𝕶 𝖙	Kk	𝖂 𝖜	Ww
𝕷 𝖑	Ll	𝖃 𝖝	Xx
𝕸 𝖒	Mm	𝖄 ü	Yy
𝕹 𝖓	Nn	Ʒ ʒ	Zz

Fraktur letters

2

Greek alphabet

Aα	Alpha	**N**ν	Nu
Bβ	Beta	Ξξ	Xi or Si
Γγ	Gamma	**O**o	Omicron
Δδ	Delta	Ππ	Pi
Eε	Epsilon	**P**ρ	Rho
Zζ	Zeta	Σσς	Sigma
Hη	Eta	**T**τ	Tau
Θθ	Theta	**Y**υ	Upsilon
Iι	Iota	Φφ	Phi
Kκ	Kappa	**X**χ	Chi
Λλ	Lambda	Ψψ	Psi
Mμ	Mu	Ωω	Omega

Cyrillic alphabet

Аа	Az	**Рр**	Rzy	
Бб	Buki	**Сс**	Slovo	
Вв	Vyedi	**Тт**	Tvyerdo	
Гг	Glagol	**Уу**	U	
Дд	Dobro	**Фф**	Fiert	
Ее	Yest	**Хх**	Kher	
Жж	Zhivete	**Цц**	Zy	
Зз	Zemlya	**Чч**	Cha	
Ии	Ishe	**Шш**	Sha	
Йй	Ishe s Kratkoi	**Щщ**	Shcha	
Кк	Kako	**Ъъ**	Tvyerdi Znak	
Лл	Lyudi	**Ыы**	Yeri	
Мм	Myslete	**Ьь**	Myakhi Znak	
Нн	Nash	**Ээ**	E	
Оо	On	**Юю**	Yu	
Пп	Pakoi	**Яя**	Ya	

2

Initial teaching alphabet

This alphabet is used in teaching children to read and is based upon the principle of 'one sound, one letter'. The alphabet is shown here with the equivalent sounds of the letters. The capital letter forms are identical to the lower case.

æ	ale	j	joy	ʃh	ship
ɑ	father	k	kit	ʒ	vision
a	at	l	lip	t	tap
au	author	m	man	th	thin
b	but	n	net	th	then
c	cat	ŋ	sing	ue	due
ch	chat	œ	toe	u	up
d	dog	o	on	v	van
ee	eel	ω	book	w	wet
e	egg	ꭣ	food	wh	why
f	fit	ou	out	y	yell
g	gun	oi	oil	ꙅ	is
h	hat	p	pig	z	fez
ie	tie	r	run		
i	ink	s	sad		

Presentation from the author (soft copy)

With the rapid advances in technology allowing more computer power for less cost, increasing numbers of authors/writers have their own personal computer enabling them to produce their copy in electronic (soft) form. This has obvious technical and commercial attractions, since it eliminates having to rekey the text before typesetting it.

However, as with hard copy, the author needs to be advised of certain practical facts.

The disk containing the electronic files should be labelled giving details of the software programs and the particular version used.

All disks sent should be write protected (locked) and should be clearly marked as to their content and ownership.

Disks should only contain files required for the job in question.

The disk should be accompanied by a hard copy proof.

A back-up copy should be kept of all material sent.

IBM to Apple

Many graphic arts dtp and typesetting systems are based on Apple Macs whereas the majority of personal computers used in the business environment are IBM based. Although originally this caused compatibility problems, the situation has eased as systems have become more open. One of the big steps in this direction occurred following the decision by Apple, IBM and Motorola to undertake a joint venture to develop the Risc-based Power PC processor. This is now being used by both Apple and IBM in their workstations offering not only an increasingly more open environment but also significantly more power although it is worth noting that only application software which has been specifically written for the PowerPC is capable of taking full advantage of the higher productivity.

Other developments which are overcoming compatibility problems include Adobe's Acrobat cross-platform electronic document software. This enables users to read, navigate and print fully formatted digital documents from the computer system of their choice. Using Portable Document Format files, the essential look of the document is preserved regardless of the hardware platform, operating system, application software or typefaces used to create the original.

In these circumstances, some of the more complicated routines described on these pages are increasingly becoming unnecessary.

Electronic (soft) copy preparation

Soft copy text can be produced in one of two ways. Either:

☐ as straight text which is then typographically formatted by a desktop publishing or typesetting system or

☐ as text and codes in order automatically to generate some or all of the typographic and page layout functions needed when the text is photoset.

Preparing the files

Whether or not it is desirable to include a degree of typographic coding as well as the word string depends upon what arrangements it is possible to make in advance, the economics of it, and what view is taken of the likely consistency and accuracy of the keyboarding which will be received.

Where no pre-planning at all has been possible and a disk just arrives with no accompanying documentation, it may be usable, but the conversion to phototypesetting is likely to be relatively expensive unless the text is very straightforward. This is because, unless the typesetter knows exactly which software, including the version (and the typefaces), was used and is able to match them, it may be necessary to reformat the text. Such an operation can take time.

Where some pre-planning is possible and the keyboard operator can be relied upon to be consistent, much better use may be made of direct interfacing by incorporating not only the words but also some agreed basic codings - 'main text size', 'heading type A', heading type B', 'extract size type', etc. - within the word string. Instead of being a completely manual task, the 'code conversion' function then becomes semi-automatic, with all the basic transfers made through a search and replace program, leaving only the more difficult formatting decisions to the operator at the editing and correction terminal.

At the most thorough end of pre-planning, a complete 'generic coding' system applied at keyboard stage will allow a fully automatic 'search and replace' routine to take place, and thus permit direct photosetting from the keystrokes.

A number of standard coding schemes have been introduced, of which the most commonly used is SGML (Standard Generalised Markup Language). Another is ASPIC (Authors' Symbolic Prepress Interfacing Codes) which is endorsed by the BPIF.

Copy transfer

The transfer of text from author to typesetter can be achieved in one of these four ways:

Direct compatibility. The disks holding the digital files are inserted into the photosetter and output with little or no intervention.

OCR. With Optical Character Recognition, the already typed or printed text is scanned and entered into the typesetting system in digital form. Originally, the print had to be in an OCR-readable typeface, but the new scanners can read almost any typewritten or printed character.

Media conversion. A media converter reads the data off the disk and translates it into a format suitable for the typesetting system.

Datacommunications/telecommunications. A data or telecommunications link is set up between the input equipment and the phototypesetting system and the data is digitally transferred. The link can either be direct or be via the public telephone network.

Direct compatibility

Much vested interest originally went into keeping systems incompatible. Some manufacturers did introduce software which enabled disks produced on other manufacturers' equipment to be output by their devices, but it was not until Adobe's PostScript became an industry standard that it became generally available. Basically, PostScript like Hewlett-Packard's PCL and Xerox's Interpress is a page description language which provides a method of communication between computers and output devices including laser printers and typesetters. In other words, it converts computer stored data into typeset quality whatever the output device.

Even so, when transferring digital text stored on a disk from an input to an output device similar practical rules apply as those given to authors.

The disk containing the electronic files should be labelled giving details of the software programs and the particular version used.

All disks sent should be write protected (locked) and should be clearly marked as to their content and ownership.

Disks should only contain files required for the job in question.

The disk should be accompanied by a hard copy proof.

A back-up copy should be kept of all material sent.

It should also be noted that:

Any fonts used should be the same version, name and manufacturer as those of the typesetter.

A separate floppy disk containing disk maintaining software should be included where appropriate.

It is essential to work to the same parameters as the typesetter. Ask if any notes or guidelines covering those areas most likely to cause problems are available.

OCR

Optical character recognition became popular when there was no other way of eliminating rekeying. However, in those days the OCR print-out operation had to be done with care, since the accuracy rate was relatively low. Since then the technology has improved considerably and almost any typewritten or printed character can be read.

Also, with some OCR software artificial intelligence is used to 'learn' as it recognises, using information gathered from clean sections of text to help interpret hard-to-read areas. As the software accumulates knowledge of a typeface, the character recognition process accelerates and becomes more accurate. Accuracy is further enhanced by lexical analysis, the automatic checking of each character for context and sequence within a word.

However, other methods of transferring text have also improved significantly and new ones have been introduced. Consequently, OCR is now mainly used for handling work which has already been typed or printed, such as where out of print texts need to be recaptured for reprinting or publishing afresh in a new format: it is still the only technology available for this which eliminates rekeyboarding.

With this technology data structured in one format is converted into a new format which will be comprehensible to a particular phototypesetting system. It is done by a media converter, a microcomputer which can be programmed to read the structure and content of a specific disk and to translate that content into the form required to obtain the information into the phototypesetting system. It can achieve this either by reading the first disk and writing a second, typesetter compatible disk; or it can read the first disk and translate/transmit the data by direct cable to the typesetting system.

First generation media converters, or 'black boxes' as they were known, required the user to do a considerable amount of the code-conversion programming and were really not viable on a one-off job basis. This problem was overcome by the next generation of systems which offered wide ranges of conversion programs and resulted in a number of bureaus being set up offering media-conversion services on a commercial basis, specifying which disks they could read and which phototypesetting outputs they could offer: where changes are made to the software the disk conversion program has to be rewritten.

However, basically it was a technology developed to overcome the problem of having no industry-wide compatibility standards including computer floppy disks and is now becoming obsolete.

Media conversion

Unlike the computer and disk manufacturers, communications suppliers recognised early the importance of compatibility taking the RS232 connector pin as the standard for connecting one electronic device to another. The contents of a computer file, whether on the hard disk in the computer or on a floppy disk played out through a RS232 port, come out sequentially, without reference to the complicated way in which the data is physically arranged on the disk. The complex deciphering of disk struc-

Data communication

ture necessary in media conversion (see above) is therefore avoided.

For transferring text any distance, you need either

☐ a network or

☐ telecommunications.

Networks

Compared with a direct cable connection between the input and the output device, networks link a number of workstations, enabling data storage units and output devices to be shared. They also enable much larger digital files to be passed between the devices at high speed and without any manual intervention.

Networks come in two forms: Local Area Networks (LANs) for internal communications within a building or a site, and Wide Area Networks (WANs) which are used to interconnect remote sites and can involve using microwave and satellite technology as well as telephone lines.

Telecommunications

Digital data can be transmitted over a standard dial-up telephone line by the use of an acoustic coupler or modem (devices which convert digital signals into audible tones for land-line transmission). The acoustic coupler is smaller, cheaper and simpler than a modem but is also slower and less accurate.

Until recently, the best way to reduce the risk of data corruption was to use a dedicated 'tied' line, such as British Telecommunications Kilostream, which can link different buildings in a town, across the country or even across continents, operating at between 64 Kbits to 1Mbit. However, it is really only economically viable if a lot of communications traffic over an extended period is envisaged, particularly following the introduction of British Telecom's Integrated Services Digital Network (ISDN).

This is a digital exchange line which allows users to send and receive high volumes of voice, data, text and image via a single digital connection across the public telephone network. It is also less likely to suffer interference or corruption than an analogue line. It is a dial-up service and calls are charged on a usage basis only: costs are less than the conventional line due to the speed, volumes and reliability that can be achieved. Each channel has a minimum capacity of up to 64 Kbits which is roughly equivalent to the transfer volume of 60 pages of A4 text in 30 seconds. It is not only available across the UK but also has worldwide links.

Compatibility problems still exist however between rival ISDN cards and it is wise to check details of the receiving card before attempting transmission.

Conversion problems

Note that there are a number of complications in media conversion.

1. Separate programs need to be written for any one specific WP to be converted to any one manufacturer's phototypesetting system

2. Where changes are made to WP software (which they frequently are), the disk conversion program has to be rewritten

3. With earlier models of 'black box' the conversion routines are fixed and cannot be modified by the user where necessary.

Casting off and copyfitting

Casting off

Casting off is the calculation of the number of pages a given amount of copy will make when set in a given typeface and size to a given type area.

There are two stages:

☐ calculating the number of characters and spaces in the copy
☐ calculating the number of characters and spaces per page of the intended setting.

1 divided by 2 then gives the answer. If the copy is in digital form the computer will normally provide the two figures automatically. If, however, it is hard copy the following is necessary.

Stage 1

Determine whether the copy is good (evenly typed, few corrections, etc.) or bad (inconsistently typed, many handwritten corrections, etc.).

Bad copy

There is no short cut possible. Bad copy needs to be counted for words, page by page, chapter by chapter. Total words x 6 = total number of characters. Add 5% to this total to allow for the spaces which will occur at the end of paragraphs with short lines when the copy is typeset. The final figure is the total number of characters and spaces in the copy.

Good copy

This can be averaged. Draw a pencil line down each sheet of copy at the end of an average line length. The 'mass' of copy can then be calculated by the sum: number of lines x number of characters and spaces in the average line. To this total must be added the few characters beyond the line, and subtracted those few finishing before the line *except* para lines. (It can be safely assumed that there will be as many spaces at the end of short lines finishing paragraphs in the copy as in the typeset version.) The final figure is therefore the total of all the characters and spaces in the manuscript folio. The total of all folios calculated in this way is the total of characters and spaces in the job. Note that typewriter and WP printer character widths will normally be either 10-to-the-inch (pica), 12-to-the-inch (elite), or 15-to-the-inch (microelite). So if, for example, the pencil line is at 6" and there are 35 lines per folio, the 'mass' will be 6x10x35 characters if a pica typewriter face has been used. Special typewriter rulers are helpful here. If a proportionately spaced typewriter or computerised word processor has been used, the average number of characters occurring per inch or per line needs first to be assessed.

Stage 2

Take the typographical specification in terms of lines of main text setting per page intended, measure intended, and the typeface and type size chosen.

Consult the appropriate cast-off tables, available from each manufacturer for his own system. The tables will yield the number of characters to the measure in your chosen type style. Hence, lines per page x this figure = total number of characters and spaces per typeset page.

Stage 1 total divided by this page total then yields the number of pages in the job. Add to this total whatever extra copy is needed such as prelims and endmatter for books.

Note also the following:

☐ always work to the *exclusive* type area (i.e. exclusive of headline, whiteline and foot folio)
☐ if copy is divided into chapters, allow half a page per chapter for chapter breaks if the specification allows for chapters to commence new pages. Alternatively, for maximum accuracy, cast off each chapter individually.

Approximate cast-off

If cast-off tables are unavailable or a specific typeface has not been chosen, an approximate cast-off can still be made. Assume the average width of character in the typeface proposed for the typeset version to be half the point size specified. Then the number of characters per line in your chosen measure will be the measure in picas x 12 divided by half the point size. Add to this figure 9% as an allowance for the fact that most typefaces have a set width less than even and that word spacing will normally be less than one en of set which this calculation otherwise allows.

Having calculated the number of characters and spaces per typeset line in this way, the rest of the cast-off calculation is as described on the previous page.

By example, this approximate calculation yields for a 10pt typeface to a measure of 24 picas (24x12) divided by (5) = (57.6) x 1.09= 62.8 characters. In practice, 10pt Baskerville set Linotron 202 (for example) yields 61 characters; 10pt Linotron Times yields 63 characters; 10pt Linotron Plantin yields 64 characters - and so on. The theoretical calculation is normally near enough to be practicable.

Copyfitting

Copyfitting is the calculation of the type size necessary in order to set a given amount of copy in a predetermined area.

As with casting off, if the copy is in digital form, copyfitting can be done automatically using most page-makeup software. These are the stages in the calculation for hard copy originals:

☐ calculating the number of characters and spaces in the copy
☐ calculating the appropriate type size to yield sensible leading, and hence fit all copy.

Stage 1

See under *Casting off* earlier in this section. Obtain thereby the character count of the manuscript.

Stage 2

Convert to picas the given depths and widths of the predetermined area.

☐ Start with 10pt of the typeface to be chosen and find from the appropriate set of cast-off tables the number of characters yielded by the measure of the predetermined area.

☐ Calculate, by dividing (character count of manuscript) by (characters of typesetting per line), the number of lines of 10pt the manuscript will yield if set solid.

☐ Calculate the depth, in points, that this number of lines will make.

☐ Calculate the additional leading necessary, if any, to fill the space vertically.

☐ If this first (10pt) trial gives an unsatisfactory result, start again with a larger or smaller type size as necessary and continue by trial and error until a satisfactory combination of type size and leading is reached.

Note that more than one solution will always be mathematically possible, so several trials may in any case be prudent before you fix upon a final specification. For example, 400 words of copy to fit into an area 50 picas deep x 20 picas wide will fit equally well if set Monotype Lasercomp Times New Roman 11/12pt, or 10/13pt, or 9/15pt - so the visual effect to be achieved must always be taken strongly into consideration.

3 Typesetting and Desk top publishing

Output devices

The traditional conventions for compartmentalizing the analysis of typesetting and composition techniques into types of process and categories of system have become largely irrelevant with the introduction of powerful micro-computers capable of controlling sophisticated off-the-shelf programs used by amateurs and professionals alike. We have therefore concentrated on explaining processes rather than preserving or devising classifications of system.

There is, however, some merit in retaining the conventional classification of output devices into 'generations' and considering these first, since the possibility of text and graphic manipulation at the 'front end' is in large measure determined by the technology of the output system.

Four generations of photosetting output devices are usually defined. These are:

Photosetting and laser technologies

☐ first generation: mechanical
☐ second generation: electro-mechanical
☐ third generation: CRT (cathode ray tube)
☐ fourth generation: laser.

First generation machines

First generation machines were derived directly from hot metal casting mechanisms. A set of film matrices (negatives) and a light source replace a set of brass matrices and the type metal mould, but in most other respects the principles for keyboarding and output remain the same.

Early machines were:

☐ Monophoto Mark I-V derived from the Monotype system

□ Intertype Fotosetter and Fotomatic derived from hot metal Intertypes.

This generation of machines is now obsolete.

Second generation machines

Second generation machines employ electronic principles to reduce mechanical movements and so increase ouput speeds.

The general principle of second generation machines is that the characters are exposed on to film or bromide paper by flashing a synchronized light source through a negative master. The masters may be carried on a revolving disk, or drum, or quadrant, according to the manufacturer's design. A lens system controls the type size required.

This generation of machine may still be in use, in a few small typesetting installations, but technologically it has been superseded by third and fourth generation machines, and can be expected soon to disappear from the scene altogether.

Common models included:

□ Itek Quadritek (quadrant)

□ A-M Comp/Edit series – earlier models (engraved disk)

□ Compugraphic Editwriter series (negative strips around drum)

□ Dymo/Photon Pacesetter (drum)

□ Monophoto 2000 system (engraved disk)

□ Mergenthaler Linotype VIP (engraved disk).

Third generation machines

By the third generation, photosetting machines moved completely away from the second generation principle of a light source flashed through a physical negative image of the character required.

In third generation technology, the design details of each character in a type fount are held digitally in computer store and generated electronically on a CRT screen.

Floppy disks provided by each manufacturer contain the digital information for any given typeface and this is read into the operating memory of the

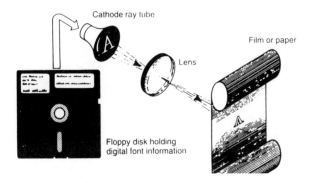

Cathode ray tube

Film or paper

Lens

Floppy disk holding
digital font information

photosetting system either when required, or is left to reside semi-permanently. When the photo unit receives a computer signal to set a particular character, an electron beam moves over the phosphor surface of a CRT screen, in a series of vertical lines, 1000 or more to the inch, to form the appropriate pattern for the character.

The imaging system of a third generation cathode ray tube typesetting machine.

The images thus formed, character by character and line by line, are projected through a fixed lens system on to bromide paper or film to produce the required text.

Point sizes were commonly specified in fractional increments, and leading adjusted to similarly fine tolerances. Type could be electronically modified by condensing, expanding or slanting characters at will.

Some typesetting systems still in general use have third generation photosetting units, although, again, they are rapidly being replaced by the latest technology. They include:

☐ Linotype-Hell's CRTronic series and Linotron 202
☐ Autologic's APS-5
☐ Scangraphic's Scantex 1000 system
☐ Agfa's (Compugraphic's) MCS 8000 series.

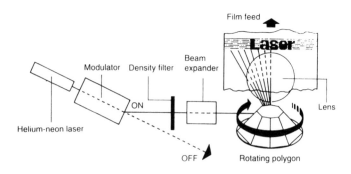

The imaging system of a fourth generation laser imagesetter

Fourth generation machines

As in third generation CRT machines, all fount information is stored within the computer memory, but the method of imaging is completely different: a laser is employed to build up the required character components with microscopic dots which are exposed directly on to the bromide paper or film in a series of sweeps defined by the computer.

Whereas third-generation CRT machines expose type letter by letter in a series of vertical lines, laser setters sweep across the full measure being set, building up the complete image scan line by scan line.

In order to set a complete page or block of text, the computer in a laser setter must therefore be given a complete layout or *bitmap* of the page in digital form before it begins to output. The unit which performs this task and drives the laser is the RIP – *raster image processor.*

These are a vital link in the imagesetting chain since they are placed between the page assembly workstation and the imagesetter, and affect productivity and quality. Available in software and hardware forms, they interpret the data which, being in PostScript, describes all the elements in a page - text, fonts, vector lines, shapes and halftones - their position and overlay priorities. The rips convert everything into raster format, as well as screen the continuous tone data and provide four colour separated images of the page at desired angles and screen rulings before outputting them to the imagesetter.

Because of the flexibility in positioning dots that this method of imaging gives, it is possible to 'type-set' any image which can be defined in a bitmap: halftones, for example. To underline this capability, laser typesetters are often (and more accurately) called laser *imagesetters*.

Resolutions start from around 900 and can go up to over 6000 dots per inch (*dpi*) – also called lines per inch (*lpi*) when scan *lines* are the measure – and setting speeds tend to be much faster than CRT machines.

In fact, from the early models, imagesetters have developed significantly, particularly in terms of accuracy and repeatability, thus enabling four colour separations to be reproduced. It has also meant that a number of different screening techniques has been introduced, particularly FM (frequency modulated) or, as some call it, stochastic screening, which aims to reduce or eliminate classical screening problems such as moire and rosette patterns, colour shift and screen clash and which, since screening is part of the rip's operation has become possible owing to the increased power of modern computers.

Stochastic screening differs from conventional screening in that, instead of using a variable dot size and a fixed frequency, it produces a fixed (or in some cases a variable) dot size and a variable spatial frequency.

This type of screening is not suitable for all laser imagesetters which basically fall into three categories: capstan drive, and internal and external drum. Tending to be less expensive and slower than other imagesetters, capstan driven devices normally use red sensitive material and are normally up to A2 in size. Examples include Agfa's AccuSet and Autologic's APS-6 ranges, plus Linotype-Hell's Linotronic 260, 330 and 560.

Internal drum imagesetters also mostly use red sensitive material but are some of the fastest machines around as well as having tight register tolerances. Despite this, they can usually handle formats up to B1. In other words, these devices can output up to 16 fully imposed pages to view or four colour separated pages. Some of the more popular internal drum machines include Agfa's SelectSet and Avantra ranges, Linotype-Hell's Herkules, as well as Scangraphics' and Scitex's ranges.

For the largest formats external drum imagesetters tend to be used, handling either red or blue sensitive material. They usually have optimum register tolerances and a wide range of speeds. Such devices are available from Optronics, Linotype-Hell, Hyphen and Barco Graphics, among others.

Laser printers

Laser printers use broadly the same raster image processing as imagesetters although originally their use for graphic arts applications was limited by low output resolutions. The most common office models (such as the Hewlett Packard Laserjet III series and the Apple LaserWriter) output at 300 dpi, giving the typographic image a characteristic 'jaggy' edge.

Higher output machines are now proliferating, however, the resolution ranging from 600 up to 2400 dpi. These laser printers (or 'plain paper imagesetters', as the higher resolution models tend to be called) are suitable for CRC reproduction as well as for proofing and direct imaging of polyester printing plates.

High speed electronic printers such as the Xerox DocuTechs are also bringing office and printing operations closer together (see Section 6).

Strike-on composition

'Strike-on composition' or 'cold type' were the terms used, before word processing and desktop publishing became part of the graphic arts scene, to describe typewriter setting - either manual fixed-space or electronic variable-space as with IBM Selectric 'golfball' setting.

By this definition the term is pretty much obsolete, since electronic printer output is now the more normal for this type of work.

Fixed-space typewriter setting

'Fixed-space' typewriter setting is normally excluded from serious typographical consideration, and standard mechanical or electric typewriters are fairly well obsolete anyway, but for printed matter which need not have pretensions to typography and where a word processing or DTP facility is absent, typewriter setting can still suffice.

The following are the standard fixed-space typewriter categories:

□ Pica (10 characters to the inch, one-sixth of an inch body depth)
□ Elite (12 characters to the inch, one-sixth of
□ an inch body depth)
□ Microelite (15 characters to the inch, one-sixth of an inch body depth).

These type size definitions - and their dimensions - have been carried forward into the WP areas too.

IBM setting

IBM Selectric typewriter setting has become more or less obsolete in competition with word processing, DTP, or the cheaper and simply installed stand-alone photosetting systems. In case replacement patches or strip lines need setting, and a system is available, you may find the following notes helpful for reference.

Quality

The IBM proportional spacing system is based on nine units that permit seven different letter widths. This is well behind the standards of normal photosetting typography.

There are only three 'escapements' to cover all designs from 7pt up to 12pt:

□ 6, 7, 8pt sizes (blue)
□ 9, 10pt sizes (yellow)
□ 11, 12pt sizes (red).

It follows that where two point sizes in the same typeface share the same escapement, then the smaller of the two is rather loosely fitted and generally less successful.

Designs which work particularly well are:

□ 10pt and 12pt Aldine (derived from Bembo)
□ 11pt Baskerville

☐ 11pt Journal (derived from Sabon)
☐ 10pt and 11pt Press Roman (derived from Times)
☐ 11pt Theme (derived from Optima).

Most suited to. . .

☐ straightforward, uniform text requiring few changes of size or weight
☐ work from in-house installations producing short-take publicity, stationery, brochures, etc.
☐ on-the-spot production of CRC for illustration labels, diagram labels, etc, where other work is proceeding meantime and no delays in film processing disrupt work flow.

Less suited to. . .

☐ work where any large degree of correction is anticipated. Corrections in IBM can only feasibly be done manually by cut-and-paste, which in volume is laborious to do and is unlikely to result in a good quality of final CRC
☐ work where there is a significant number of changes in typeface, type size or type weight. Each change to bold, italic, etc., stops the machine and requires an operator to intervene in order to change the golf ball.

Daisy-wheel printer output

Daisy-wheel printers operate on the 'strike-on' principle. The characters are arranged around the outside of a petal-shaped disk and a character is printed out when the petal head carrying it is hammered on to the printer ribbon and against the paper behind.

Because of the mechanical constraints involved, daisy-wheel printers are the slowest of the printer types available: most print out at around 35-60cps.

Most daisy-wheel printer founts are fixed-format, fixed-space founts, based on the standard manual or electric typewriter faces (Courier, Gothic, etc.) and produce crisp, clearly defined characters which are very much to the full 'letter-quality' specification. The very best results are obtained when a carbon film printer ribbon is used with a metallized (rather than plastic) print wheel.

Some manufacturers – notably Diablo and Qume – offer a number of attractive daisy-wheel faces with proportional spacing characteristics.

Dot-matrix printer output

Dot-matrix printers imprint the image of a character on paper by selecting from a vertical matrix of pins on the printing head the appropriate patterns to form the shape of the letter required. It follows that the more pins that are used to form the letter, the denser the letter, and the crisper the image. The original conventional dot-matrix printer has a 9-pin head, and so prints out relatively unrefined letter shapes with a low level of density. The more modern and possibly more expensive models have more pins per head, and so offer a very much greater level of clarity and density. Many of these models offer two forms of printout quality: draft mode, which is a high speed operating mode using less than the full number of pins; and Near Letter Quality (NLQ) mode, which offers a good level of image. Likewise, the same models offer a choice of typefaces, including proportionally spaced founts as well as fixed space founts.

For reproduction purposes, the NLQ mode gives passable repro quality; and as long as typographical expectations are not too high, this can be quite a practical option.

Text input

There have been varied and numerous methods over the years for managing the input of text to a system which can justify lines of type or compose pages but for the practical purposes of this book we will ignore those which have faded into obsolescence and concentrate on methods which are contemporary or are still in use.

The different approaches to data capture comprise:

☐ keyboarding by a professional typesetter from the hard copy of the typescript

☐ scanning hardcopy by an optical character recognition device

☐ using digital files to 'import' into the imagesetting system either directly or through one of a series of conversion methods.

Proprietary keyboards

All manufacturers of typesetting equipment have in the past manufactured their own keyboards. There were many reasons why conventional microprocessor or computer terminals could not be used for this purpose. Two of the most significant problems were that such 'general' keyboards were unable to access the range of characters and commands necessary to achieve justified text with all its complexities and such keyboards did not have the resilience necessary for constant high speed use.

This has changed, as we shall see, although a few 'professional' keyboards may still be in use in the typesetting industry especially where high level mathematical and scientific setting is concerned. The original typesetting input terminals had little or no display. The keyboard operator would key text into the system without being able to see on a display the eventual results of his work.

As computing power and sophistication increased, larger and larger displays were added to keyboard terminals (and in due course it became possible to see the characteristics of the typefaces being created) until the distinction between an input terminal and a terminal capable of manipulating text and making up pages became quite blurred.

The generation of input devices before those which displayed the characteristics of the made up page effectively captured 'straight' text which was later passed to a more sophisticated system for making into pages or output as columns of type for cutting and pasting into position.

Many of these terminals were code-driven, which means that the typographical instructions, rather than be interpreted in such a way that the typeface is seen on the screen, are input in the form of codes and these codes remain embedded in the text (visually as well as in the computer's memory) until they are reinterpreted into typefaces at the output stage.

It is possible for a competent keyboarder handling large volumes of straight text to achieve very high speeds using a code-driven system, especially when the number of size and fount changes is relatively small.

Code-driven systems often have the facility to store *user definable formats* (*UDF*) which can combine frequently recurring typographic instruction sequences under a single code. This can reduce the complication of keyboarding complicated typography.

Keyboards which have been adapted or were purpose-built to drive a typesetting system usually have a larger range of keys than a conventional personal computer or word processor and this can also speed up the creation of text since it implies fewer keystrokes to obtain special characters (which through a 'general' keyboard can sometimes only be obtained by using a combination of several keys at once).

This was particularly useful when heavy mathematical and scientific setting was involved, where large numbers of special characters (*special sorts*) were in use and where these could be accessed directly from the keyboard without the need to remember large numbers of special key combinations.

Those typesetters who specialized in mathematical typesetting used to have special keyboards with very large numbers of keys designed specifically for this purpose. The disadvantage of such large keyboard layouts was, of course, that it was difficult to key as fast over a wide range of keys as with a small, compact layout. However, more powerful hardware and software has now obviated the need for such complex keyboard layouts.

Optical character recognition

Optical character recognition (OCR) machines had been in use in data processing departments and in banking (for the reading of cheques) for 20 years or so before they were taken up by the typesetting industry.

An OCR device operates by scanning a beam of light across a page of copy; the optical signals reflected from each character in the copy are analysed and compared with a corresponding master image of characters contained in the unit's memory. As each character is 'recognized' it is converted into digital codes which can then be passed to the typesetting system and become text within the system's memory.

Early machines were both expensive and limited in the small number of typefaces they could read. The first commercial machines were designed to be able to read one typewriter face (Courier 12) and two special computer-generated typefaces known as *OCR A* and *OCR B*. Such machines were therefore useful if there was control over the typeface being used to create the typescript, but of course in such circumstances it was commonly possible to arrange for the text to be keyed straight into a computer in any event.

As computers became more powerful it was possible to 'train' OCR readers to recognize a wide variety of typefaces and in due course to work out the characteristics of an unknown typeface by a trial and error process of making guesses which were then corrected on some sample text by an operator.

The best known of these 'transitional' machines is the Kurzweil data entry machine which was the first OCR to make a steady inroad into typesetting input. Today there are a number of intelligent OCR devices which can recognize a wide range of typefaces, either typewritten or printed and they include hand-held devices which can be manually passed across the face of a sheet of typewriting to convert this into computer code.

There are also a number of low cost software packages which can be run on personal computers and work directly with popular input scanners. Other developments include the use of artificial intelligence to 'learn' as the software recognizes, using information gathered from clean sections of text to help interpret hard-to-read areas, and so become more accurate and faster. Then there is lexical analysis, the automatic checking of each character for context and sequence within a word, as well as neural network technology which has improved the recognition of degraded documents.

There are many applications where such OCR machines are very useful but there are areas worth checking out.

For example, handwritten editing on the typescript can confuse some OCR readers into misreading the typewritten characters. Also, what is the percentage accuracy in reading not only the cleanest, specially prepared typescript but also not so clean material? It is one of the paradoxes of typesetting that to insert corrections into previously typeset text can often take as long as rekeying the text itself.

In fact, OCR is most productive when it is possible to present the device with clean, well prepared typescript or printed material where the OCR reader can achieve a success rate of a hundred percent (or close to it) in interpreting the text. Again, where such circumstances exist, it may equally well be possible to key directly into a computer file which avoids the need for reinterpretation at all.

However, there are several instances where text has already been keyed and it is cost-effective to recapture in digital form this information. A common example is that of a large printed volume where the typesetting files are no longer available, either because they have been misplaced or because the book was originally created before it was customary or possible to keep electronic files of typeset material. In such a circumstance, OCR can be a very cost-effective method of recapturing the text in digital form.

Word processing

As word processing programs became more sophisticated and proprietary typesetting input systems more 'user friendly' the distinction between the two has disappeared for all but the most sophisticated work.

There are, however, some problems remaining since word processing programs are still in use by office staff, authors and journalists of a generation before the latest, typographical based programs became available. There also remain potential incompatibilities between some standard word processing programs and the devices and software which are going to interpret their text into typesetting. Let us look at some of these potential problems.

First, the physical transfer, since there is no industry standard for floppy disks - the medium most commonly used by word processing systems and by personal computers. Some of the varying factors are as follows:

- ☐ size: 3" 31/2" 51/4" or 8"
- ☐ no. of sides: single or double
- ☐ recording density: single, double or quad
- ☐ sectoring: hard or soft
- ☐ formatting: differing arrangement of information on the disk surface
- ☐ recording speed: some disks revolve at different speeds depending on which areas are being read.

All these and other physical discrepancies must be handled in such a way that data can be presented to the typesetting system in a uniform and consistent manner.

We have already noted that original personal computer keyboards may need special combinations of keystrokes to generate the range of characters necessary for typesetting. There must therefore be software which can convert these code combinations to formats understandable by the typesetting system. Indeed, the actual coding system used to store the textual information in the computer's memory may itself be different from that used by the typesetting system and this in turn must be interpreted.

The problems become multiplied by factors which are necessary to stipulate in typesetting but have no meaning in older generations of word processing: typeface, size, interlinear space, justification mode, fixed spaces, opening and closing quotes, and so on.

And all these requirements are separate from, and in addition to, the basic fact that early word processing programs had no access to typeface founts and therefore to distinguish one typeface from another special codes must be inserted in the file which can then be reinterpreted by the typesetting system.

At this stage it is worth taking a brief look at methods of coding.

Basically, it is possible to code text for later reinterpretation by a computer in two ways: either the typographic characteristics can be coded directly (e.g. you might have a code of T1 for Times Roman, S8 for size = 8 point, L 10 for leading equals 10 point, M23 for measure = 23 picas, and so on) or you can code elements of structure which can later be interpreted into typography by a translation system within the typesetting process (for example, H1 may indicate heading level 1 which may in turn be reinterpreted by the typesetting system which understands that all level 1 headings should be in 18 point Times bold set left, and so on).

The first type of coding is termed *typographic* and the second is termed *generic*.

Generic coding is potentially much more flexible than typographic coding since the process of identifying structure means that the codes can be used for purposes additional to typographic instruction if required – for example, to allocate fields to different elements of structure within a database. Note that there are several generic coding systems of which *standard generalized markup language* (*SGML*) is fast becoming definitive.

An example of typographic coding is that used by the early Linotype APL terminals, as explained above.

If we look at *contemporary* word processing programs, we will find a much greater compatibility between this software and text manipulation and page make-up software.

There are two reasons for this. The first is that such programs have evolved rapidly towards typographic-based systems and the second is that the contemporary page make-up software contains *filters* which automatically translate modern word processing input and can incorporate it without fuss or bother.

Most modern word processing programs running on IBM compatible, Macintosh and Unix workstations allow the user to identify typefounts, sizes and a range of typographical specifications which relate closely to the eventual output required by the page make-up software. It is possible, therefore, for the files from a word processing package like Microsoft Word to be taken directly into a page make-up program with the typography and format appearing as anticipated by the original keyboarder.

Problems of incompatibility may still occur: for example, disk formats and sizes may be different, the type of machine on which the files were created may be different (Microsoft Word can be used on both IBM compatible PCs and on Macintoshes) but even these incompatibilities may be resolved with modern hardware and software. Different sizes of disk can be handled by special disk drives and plenty of software now exists for converting one system's 'protocol' into another. For example, Apple Macintosh computers are capable of reading files created under MS DOS or Windows – the IBM PC-compatible operating system – and converting them to Macintosh language.

Things became easier still following the introduction of the PowerPC processor, the result of a joint development between Apple Computers, IBM and Motorola. This is now being used by both Apple and IBM in their workstations, offering not only an increasingly more open environment but also significantly more power, although it is worth noting that only application software which has been specifically written for the PowerPC is capable of taking full advantage of the higher productivity.

Other developments which are overcoming application software compatibility problems include Adobe's Acrobat cross-platform electronic document software. This enables users to read, navigate and print fully formatted digital documents from the computer system of their choice. Using special Portable Document Format files, the essential look of the document is preserved regardless of the hardware platform, operating system, application software or typefaces used to create the original.

Modern word processing software is therefore a popular contemporary method of inputting text into typesetting systems and all modern systems are capable of taking such files and using them.

It is also possible to link machines directly either by cable or over a telephone line and send files into the typesetting system by this method. At its most basic, such a system may comprise a number of terminals networked together with the workstations which will manage the page make-up. In fact, many modern typesetting installations comprise exactly this: a number of personal computers running entirely off-the-shelf software, word processing and desktop publishing packages, and networked together so that files may be passed around the system with ease.

Page make-up

Manual make-up

Despite the proliferation of many inexpensive and effective automatic systems for making up pages on computer screens, there are still some instances of pages of typesetting being composed by setting columns of type and then pasting these into the eventual shape of the page on a backing sheet.

Such manual make-up can be performed either with film or paper and most typesetting machines have the facility to output negative or positive film or bromide paper, or with laser printers outputting plain paper.

Illustrations can be pasted into position either as conventional film negatives or positives, or as screened bromides or PMTs.

The compositor uses a basic set of tools: typescale, scalpel, pens, possibly mechanical tints and rules and either a proprietary glue or small machine which waxes the back of the paper elements. Film make-up is more expensive than paper composition but it is possible to achieve much finer tolerances and higher quality in the final printed image. Film has a greater resolving power than conventional bromide paper, thereby achieving crisper edges to the phototypeset material, and it may be possible to use it directly for plate making, thereby avoiding an intermediary contact stage which might lose some definition.

The paper elements which make up the page are often pasted into position on grids pre-printed with blue lines which will not reproduce – *litho blue grids* – or alternatively are made up over a light box which illuminates a black grid which can be seen through the carrier sheet, thereby aiding positioning.

Photocopies of the pages can be taken from both film and bromides for proofing purposes although this has not always been the case: film used to require the more expensive diazo process to produce contact ammonia prints – ozalids, blueprints or dye lines. Blueprints do not give the same faithful impression of the eventual appearance of the printed page and are more difficult to use for checking purposes. However, they still tend to be used for final proofs of imposed sections.

Back in the mid nineteen eighties, the range of programs available to manipulate text and make-up pages looked very different. It was then not generally possible to see an exact representation on the screen of the page which would eventually be printed. As explained above, typesetting files were generally code-driven, screens showed only one monospaced fount rather than simulations of typefaces, and in so far as there were programs which made up the pages on screens, these tended to operate by allocating positions to elements, specified on a grid by a series of numeric indices.

Whether these systems would have evolved into their current shapes without outside intervention is arguable; what is certain is that it was pressure from outside the typesetting industry which gave us the significant advances in the late nineteen eighties to the point where we now have very powerful programs capable of making-up typeset pages very effectively.

The microcomputer industry rather than the typesetting industry was responsible for the leap forward and it came in the shape of something which was at the time given the marketing term *desktop publishing* which – as inappropriate as it is – has survived. There were, in fact, several innovations which occurred simultaneously to create these new systems. Firstly, low cost laser printers based on the Canon engine became widely available and offered output that was capable of reproducing typefaces as distinct from simulated typewriter founts.

Secondly, Apple had produced a computer with three outstanding characteristics: it was relatively powerful, it had an operating system which appeared to the user to be graphics-based rather than code-driven and it had a screen which showed images at a resolution capable of differentiating one typeface from another. A third advance was made by Adobe Systems in California who devised PostScript, a *page description language* which can interpret computer information in such a way that it presents to a raster image processor (rip) data formulated to describe the output of a page created by laser. And

Screen make-up

the fourth innovation was the development of PageMaker, a fairly basic (at the time) but very user friendly program which enabled word processor files to be made up into pages which showed all their elements in position on the screen in the typefaces in which they would appear when printed.

It is interesting to note that these innovations were not designed to aid the typesetting industry but were primarily advances in office technology which would facilitate the production of attractively presented documents in the commercial world: in other words, would give typesetting-like quality to office documentation.

In the event, they precipitated a technological revolution in typesetting which after a year or so of hesitation the major typesetting vendors took up and adapted for professional purposes while, at the same time, the original programs were refined and additional programs were written until the desktop publishing standards came close to those required by professional typesetters with the essential added bonus of total visual representation of eventual results – *what you see is what you get* (*WYSIWYG*) – and dramatically improved ease of use over proprietary typesetting systems.

One incidental but highly significant result of these advances was that the language used to describe the pages output – PostScript – gained such a foothold so quickly in the market place that it became a *de facto* standard where no standard had previously existed. The consequence of this has been that all major typesetting equipment manufacturers now produce machines capable of using PostScript as the page description language and high levels of compatibility between word processing, page make-up and other typesetting software have occurred within a very short space of time.

It needs to be realized though that PostScript does vary: just as there are IBM PC-compatible personal computers, there are also PostScript compatible software and hardware products. Added to which, PostScript Level 2 offers not only increased productivity over PostScript Level 1 but also device independent colour, enabling more predictable results to be created and viewed on a variety of displays and printers, and higher quality colour separations.

The vast majority of page make-up and typesetting software, together with the output devices, now conforms to the PostScript standard. Professional make-up systems themselves include desktop publishing programs and there are proprietary professional systems developed along similar lines (i.e. with WYSIWYG representation and similar ease of use) but with expanded facilities and tighter controls. We will look at some of the most popular DTP packages first.

PageMaker

As we have seen, PageMaker was the first DTP page make-up package and is one of the most widely used. Its first release had many deficiencies – especially typographical – and contained a fair number of eccentricities, but its simplicity, speed and ability to manipulate the text and graphics were so impressive that it was an instantaneous success, particularly in the office and corporate market, although insufficiently refined to be used by professionals at that stage.

Subsequent releases and especially release 5 for the Macintosh brought the program up to levels of sophistication adequate for a wide range of professional typesetting needs and began to challenge QuarkXPress in the graphic arts and designer areas. For instance, it enables colour separations to be processed from within the program; has improved kerning and tracking, and enables graphics and text to be rotated by .001 of a degree. Also, like QuarkXPress, it is possible to add additional software. Called Additions, these enable users to tailor PageMaker for specific publishing needs.

PageMaker is a particularly flexible package in the sense that – unlike most of the other major DTP programs – it does not rely on the concept of frames into which text and graphics are positioned. Instead, it extends the use of the Apple 'pasteboard' concept so that the pages being made-up appear to be mounted on a pasteboard where elements can be temporarily positioned. Text flowed onto the page takes up the

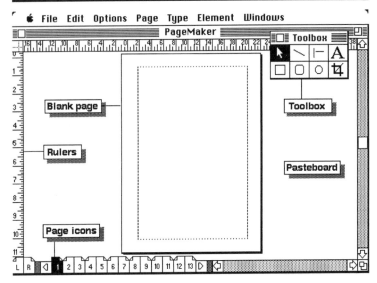

Basic elements of the PageMaker screen.

shape of the columns on the page although these columns can be manipulated in whole or in part to create different size blocks. Text links automatically from block to block and 'handles' on the blocks enable the block sizes to be repositioned and resized, vertically and horizontally with the text reformatting itself within the redefined blocks.

Both blocks and graphics can be moved very simply and the overall result is a high degree of flexibility of layout, page by page.

PageMaker is therefore primarily a page-orientated package which does not provide as high a degree of total pagination automation as some other programs intended for the creation of long documents.

PageMaker has good facilities for taking in text and graphics in common PC and Macintosh file formats, and flexible methods of linking pages back to the original files.

Text can be condensed and stretched from 5 to 250% of its original length. There is widow and orphan control and a 'keep with' facility to enable headings and body text to be treated as one element which cannot be broken.

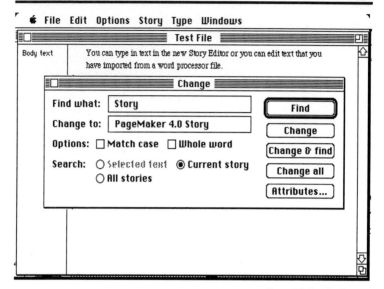

Test File

Body text   You can type in text in the new Story Editor or you can edit text that you have imported from a word processor file.

Change

Find what: **Story**

Change to: **PageMaker 4.0 Story**

Options: ☐ Match case   ☐ Whole word

Search: ○ Selected text   ◉ Current story
          ○ All stories

Find

Change

Change & find

Change all

Attributes...

The text editor contains some useful facilities such as search and replace. There is also a table editor which enables tables to be created for placing into a publication.

PageMaker's Story Editor.

Xerox Ventura Publisher

Ventura was one of the first DTP programs which could be used on the IBM PC and its compatibles – indeed, until the early nineties could only be used on these machines – and became popular partly because of this. Its first version used the Gem graphical user interface from Digital Research but the later 'Gold Edition' on the PC has versions for Gem, OS/2 and – significantly – Windows 3.0. It is also now available on the Macintosh and Unix.

Ventura is notably different from PageMaker in its approach, being both a frame-based program, where text is imported into frames set up on the page beforehand, and primarily designed for long documents, rather than flexible interactive make-up of single pages.

There are some disadvantages in the rigidity of the Ventura approach although these are really prices paid for a higher discipline of make-up of the longer documents.

For example, flowing text around irregular graphics can be problematic whereas with the page-based packages it tends to be relatively straightforward.

Style sheets are a characteristic of Ventura. Most text formatting is achieved by applying pre-defined styles to complete paragraphs. And unlike some of the other programs it can be difficult to override these to achieve unique exceptions.

The style sheets are highly effective, offering many permutations of typographical and layout characteristic, but there is quite a high overhead involved in ensuring all styles are properly and comprehensively defined before beginning work on the document. Having set styles, however, they can be applied to a range of documents, not merely the document in production at the time and with continual use it is possible to build up a library of Ventura style sheets which can cover most eventualities encountered by the average user.

If paragraph tags are embodied in the text, which can be interpreted by the program, then formatting becomes highly automated and a high degree of automatic pagination is possible.

Ventura is ideal, therefore, where there are large volumes of similar text being processed and where it is productive to spend considerable time setting up style sheets to determine formats which are likely to be repeated frequently.

Originally the text editing facilities in Ventura were limited and slow so there was little advantage in actually working on text within the program other than for a relatively limited range of corrections and adjustments.

Most of the major file formats could be imported with one or two notable exceptions. However, conditions are improving all the time. It is also possible to import text in one file format and export it in another which indicates that the program can be used for translation purposes, although on a relatively modest basis.

Probably Ventura's biggest deficiency for a document-based program has been its limited hyphenation resources. As far as the UK program is concerned, hyphenation is handled by a rule-based algorithmn and there is no access to a comprehensive dictionary. Careful manual control over hyphenation is therefore essential.

There are several third party add-ons to the program, including output driver alternatives to PostScript, for example to third generation phototypesetters which are not capable of accepting PostScript files.

QuarkXPress

QuarkXPress was originally only available in a Macintosh version but there is now a PC edition. Originally, XPress was and still is highly popular with graphic designers because although frame-based – and therefore in some respects less flexible in terms of manoeuvrability than PageMaker – it offers high degrees of typographical control and very fine increments of adjustment, enabling elements to be positioned and manoeuvred with great precision.

Early versions were arguably relatively slow to use since they set out to achieve high standards that incurred a penalty of sometimes requiring complicated sequences on the part of the operator to implement. From Version 3 the program has offered simpler methods of achieving some of the modifications to text and layout.

Boxes set up on the page are defined as containing text or graphics and text boxes can be linked so that text flows through them by chaining them together in any order specified by the operator (typically this is managed by using graphical 'chains' defined by the mouse).

From Version 3 onwards XPress offers freedom to move boxes with relative ease while maintaining the same chains between them. Version 3 also provided a pasteboard, like PageMaker, so that elements can be taken off the page for reuse elsewhere or pages can be allowed to bleed over the edge.

As in PageMaker, style sheets are provided but it is possible to override them or not use them.

Hyphenation and justification are good, and there are controls over the number of consecutive hy-

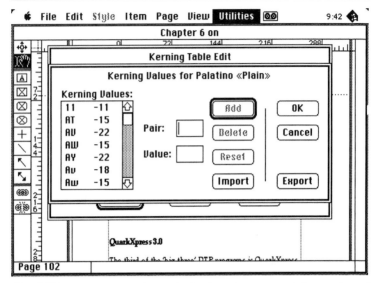

*QuarkXPress
Kerning Pairs
Editor*

phens, the hyphenation zone, minimum size of word for hyphenation and the minimum number of characters before and after the hyphen. There is also an option to prevent the breaking of capitalized words.

Kerning and tracking are highly controllable and text can be locked to a pre-defined base line grid.

Text editing facilities within QuarkXPress are good and it was one of the first DTP programs to have an effective spell checker and advanced search and replace facilities capable of being operated from within the program. One feature of the search and replace facility is the extremely valuable ability to search on text attributes such as fount and typesize and change these automatically to alternatives.

Apart from being widely used by graphic designers, it has become increasingly popular with magazine publishers and is often used for highly integrated book work where fine levels of control are necessary.

One of the reasons for the popularity of XPress among professional typesetters and publishers is the ability to add additional software (called

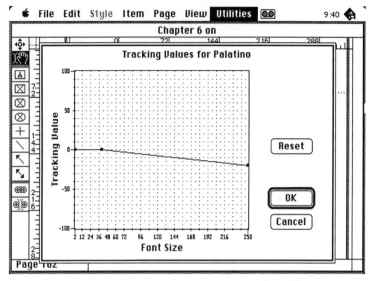

gram works) or to provide extra facilities such as automatic housekeeping routines, tracking systems and so on which enable a program to be integrated into a complete typesetting system. XPress has, in fact, been used in this context by many professional typesetting and publishing organisations to build up a complete system using the basic page make-up program and adding on other resources with Xtensions.

QuarkXPress
Tracking Editor

Letraset Ready Set Go and Design Studio

Ready Set Go was Letraset's first DTP offering and achieved some popularity in the early days although progressively failing to compete with PageMaker and QuarkXPress.

Version 4 added considerable typographic sophistication but was again leapfrogged by the two leading programs and the company started describing it as an 'office publishing system'. In 1990, however, Letraset introduced Design Studio which, although it operated in a similar way to RSG, had a much wider range of resources and facilities (particularly for the graphic designer) enabling it to compete effectively although running some way behind PageMaker and QuarkXpress in terms of units sold.

One of the interesting features of Design Studio is that it can be used in several different ways and in varying degrees of grid control or pasteboard-style freedom.

There is good control over kerning and leading, tracking and runarounds, and facilities include text rotation and the ability to condense or expand type.

Another interesting feature is the possibility of applying style sheets to characters rather than paragraphs which can be useful in graphic design work and some magazine production.

The Design Studio version of QuarkXPress Xtensions is 'Annexes', which allows the program to be customized and extended.

FrameMaker

FrameMaker was initially aimed at the technical documentation market and ran on Unix workstations. It became available on the Macintosh in 1990 and found some popularity as a professional magazine system.

It is a highly complex program, well suited to multi-user environments, but with such a range of resources and facilities that high levels of training are really necessary to enable its operators to use it effectively. It also needs powerful hardware with plenty of memory and disk space and, preferably, large monitors.

It has many features which are comparable with proprietary professional typesetting systems, including a good hyphenation dictionary, sophisticated text processing tools and, with highly effective style sheets like Design Studio, its styles can be applied to selected characters or words.

It has good facilities for the creation of long documents, as might be expected from a program which came out of technical documentation usage, but so far it has found relatively little usage among book publishers or typesetters specializing in the production of long books and this may be due to its complexity, which is comparable with professional systems tried and tested.

There are many other desktop publishing programs in use, particularly in commercial as distinct from typesetting or publishing environments, but they are generally losing ground to PageMaker, QuarkXpress and Ventura in particular.

Unlike professional typesetting systems which have a very small market and must therefore be priced quite highly, DTP packages are relatively cheap to buy and − since their development can be effectively financed by the large number of units sold − they continue to be improved and given enhanced facilities to the point where there is now little distinction between the major DTP programs and professional typesetting make-up programs at the page level.

It is probable, therefore that the distinction will cease to be particularly relevant. Meanwhile, however, there are still some specialist areas of typesetting where professional systems are still necessary as has been proved by packages such as BBZ and Page Director. In fact, this is particularly true where large volumes of pages need to be made up automatically, and it is worth looking at the type of facilities offered by such programs, which, incidentially, are often run on standard platform hardware, thus keeping costs down.

In an automatic batch pagination program all the rules for page make-up are defined in advance and input into the computer as a file of specifications

Batch pagination

against which the text is processed. Provided the program has sufficient flexibility to interpret these specifications and the hardware has sufficient power to try various permutations until the best solution is achieved, the job can be paged completely automatically.

The rules for pagination are derived from the publisher or designer, who specifies a full set of hyphenation and justification parameters plus a list of potential pitfalls to be avoided, e.g. widows, orphans, headings at bottoms of pages, and so on.

The operator defines the standard page layout: page depth, columns, measure, gutter widths, positions of folio lines, etc.

Preferences are normally given for the positioning of illustrations. Typically, they may be placed at the top, bottom or centre of the column or in position where referenced in the text. If the system is capable of handling graphics, then illustrations may be pulled in as part of the page file: otherwise white space will be left to the depth of the picture.

Where tables are involved, if tabular matter needs to be broken at the foot of a page then the system might automatically repeat the headings at the top of the next page so there is no confusion about the sequence of the table columns.

Footnotes will be automatic, capable of being contained within a single column or running across the width of the page and breaking automatically to the next page.

The system will automatically handle a hierarchy of footnote reference characters so that the editor need not mark these in. Space between footnotes and text can be defined and will be automatically created.

There will similar facilities for side notes, shoulder notes, text references, or other textual appendages to pages.

Running heads or feet would be automatically created from a file which contains the information necessary to achieve this (e.g., title of book on recto page, chapter title on verso) and page numbers will be automatically added in whatever positions the operator specifies.

Widows and orphans can be avoided and can be specified in terms of percentage of line length or by some other method as being acceptable or unacceptable.

'Keeps' – that is the facility to keep a certain number of lines with a heading before a page break and so avoid the illogicality of headings standing alone at the foot of a page – can be specified according to depth, numbers of lines, or other parameters.

Similarly other blocks of text can be specified as needing to avoid breaking at the foot of pages (e.g., tables, mathematical equations, verses of poetry). Equally, chapter endings can be specified as pages which require more than a minimum number of lines on the page to avoid the aesthetic peculiarity of a chapter ending with, say, a couple of lines at the top of the page.

Fixed amounts of space can be specified between illustrations, tables, text and captions, between footnotes and text, between paragraphs, between lines of text in equal increments, and wherever white space exists in the page in proportional increments.

Space can be specified as absolutely fixed or as variable within certain limits.

All these types of preference – and many others in the more sophisticated systems – are given priorities and the program works by making numerous attempts at pagination, firstly trying to avoid every specified item and trying to achieve optimum hyphenation and justification and then by systematically allowing the less important characteristics to default.

To achieve the best results from such systems great care is necessary in specifying parameters to ensure that reasonable integrity is maintained in page make-up while avoiding setting specifications which are mathematically impossible to accommodate.

Given sensible specifications and skilled and experienced use, batch pagination systems can run extremely fast, creating pages at a rate of a few seconds per page or, on straight text, at the rate of a few seconds per chapter.

Miles and Pentos have been notable suppliers offering these sorts of resource and Xyvision have had considerable success in developing systems which can batch paginate while allowing useful degrees of interactivity for specific adjustment of pages.

Batch pagination systems were originally run in an opaque mode, i.e. with the operator unable to see on the screen the results of the pagination. But in recent years they have adopted WYSIWYG presentations of their results so that the pages created can automatically be viewed in their typographical format.

Such systems are, of course, expensive to acquire and need considerable training and resource within the units which operate them. They are only sensible where large volumes of material need to be processed in a highly professional manner and skilled staff can be employed to make use of them.

A batch pagination system called Autopage,which has quite impressive facilities for bookwork, is available as a Quark Xtension. It is particularly strong on integrated, large format books.

Newspaper systems

The other circumstance in which large and complicated systems are appropriate is in the newspaper environment where some of the very largest dispersed systems, consisting of hundreds of terminals, are in use.

The characteristic of such newspaper systems - of which one of the best known is Atex - is that they provide editorial, managerial and financial control over the activities of the organization in addition to purely production functions.

Because of the speed and complexity of newspaper production, it is necessary to track and record the status of editorial copy at every stage, hold references to the staff creating and editing material and note times and dates, page assignments, and so on.

Additionally, special programs must handle advertisement copy both in display and in classified. These programs typically handle the financial control of the advertising as well as the make-up of individual ads and the composition of ads into pages. They will therefore log in copy, update customer accounts, issue invoices, statements and so on, and subsequently sort an issue's worth of advertisements into correct classification and sequence.

Management reports on the status of the system and aspects of the business of the newspaper (e.g., the day's advertising revenue) can then be produced from the computers.

Traditionally, such systems were based on expensive proprietory hardware, the major suppliers being Press Computer Systems, ND Comtec and Atex, which offered a wide variety of configurations ranging from a few terminals suitable for a

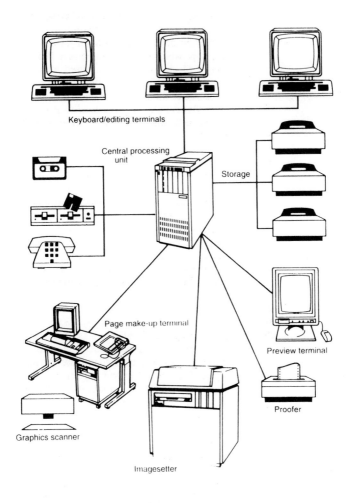

Keyboard/editing terminals

Central processing unit

Storage

Page make-up terminal

Preview terminal

Graphics scanner

Proofer

Imagesetter

Typical large on-line system

provincial weekly newspaper up to massive systems with hundreds of on-line terminals which can produce the great and famous national and metropolitan newspapers.

However, as the microcomputer became more powerful and capable of networking, newspaper publishers began to see the low-cost advantages of desktop publishing based on either IBM PCs or Apple Macintoshes. Initially used to handle the graphics and some production elements, they were then moved into the classified advertising and finally the editorial departments, allowing direct keyboarding by the journalists, as with, for example, the Quark Publishing System.

This has of course meant a significant increase in the number of workstations involved and the need for sophisticated open environment software for managing and integrating all the data, particularly as digital input devices including digital cameras and digitised libraries come on to the scene. As a result, a new type of supplier has come to the fore, that is the system integrator such as Pindar and Cascade Systems.

As will be clear from this review of the various types of graphics manipulation and page make-up possibilities, the permutations of system design are virtually limitless.

At one end of the scale it is possible to have a simple desktop publishing system with word processing and page make-up on one small personal computer and a cable linked to a laser printer – still perfectly capable of producing professional looking made-up pages – while at the other it is possible to have hundreds of terminals, a wide range of graphics input equipment (mentioned in the *Origination* section), OCR readers, and business accounting functions, capable of managing a large commercial enterprise like a daily newspaper.

It should be noted that whatever the system, the software and the hardware elements will need to be kept in balance. Large front-end systems capable of producing high volumes of pages will require extremely fast running output devices which can both handle the capacity of the front-end and interpret

the sophisticated data coming through. Equally, all
the peripherals on such systems will need to be of an
adequate standard and capacity.

4 Origination and reproduction

Presentation of hard copy originals

Originals which are viewed by reflected light (e.g. *reflection copy* [handwritten] drawn artwork, photographic prints, typematter, bromides) are known as *reflection copy*.

Originals which are viewed by transmitted light (e.g. colour transparencies, film positives) are known as *transmission copy*. *transmission copy* [handwritten]

Black and white originals [handwritten right margin]

Illustrations can be reproduced either in line or in tone depending on their nature. Where gradations of tone are a characteristic of the original, then tone reproduction is necessary; where black lines only are involved (be it in the outlines of a drawing, or in cross-hatching, or in stippling to give the illusion of tone) then line reproduction is necessary. *in the same way as text.* [handwritten]

In cases where both lines and tones are present in the original and a camera used for reproduction, either a compromise has to be reached with the line element being shot in tone together with the background or, where costs allow it, one shot can be taken for line and one for tone and, after extensive handwork, the two brought together at film or platemaking stage as a line-and-tone combination. The second option is expensive, although giving much the superior and more faithful result.

Black and white line originals (normally reflection copy)

Where you can influence this, advise the following:

☐ drawn artwork to be in black Indian ink on good quality artboard

☐ firm outlines, with any corrections made using process white paint stippling or cross-hatching not to be too fine, particularly if a significant reduction from drawn size is involved

☐ drawn in size no more than twice-up unless the thickness of line is robust enough to survive reduction beyond 50%

☐ where a line-and-tone effect is required, or a type-and-tone effect is needed, to draw or paste the line element over the tone element, in register, as an overlay (hence obviating the need for camera separation and handwork)

☐ sizing instructions to be marked carefully on the face of the artwork in non-reproducing light blue pencil.

Note also that typematter for reproduction is subject to the same comments. Take care particularly with camera-ready copy which is heavily patched. More than one depth of patch can throw a shadow on camera, and leave a 'cut line' which might find its way through to printed copies. Note also that typefaces with fine hairline serifs, such as Bodoni, are particularly demanding to reproduce.

Black and white tone originals (normally reflection copy)

These will in most cases be photographic prints.

Where you can influence the presentation of black photographic prints, specify the following:

☐ glossy bromide prints in black (not matt or embossed finish)

☐ wide tonal range but without over-strong black/white contrast

☐ avoid marks from paper clips, staples, or writing on the back in hard pencil or biro

☐ ideally to be somewhere between same-size and half-up in size in relation to the final, originated size, and size of reproduction.

Check finally to see if any retouching is necessary before reproduction.

Where you are considering the black and white reproduction of a coloured original using mechanical rather than digital processes, bear in mind the inevitable loss in clarity and contrast which will ensue when a wider range of colours is rendered as shades of grey. If in any doubt about the result, have a black and white photograph taken of the original, check this, and if satisfactory reproduce from this rather than the coloured original.

Whereas black and white and colour line originals might be reproduced by process camera, coloured tone originals are more likely to be scanned. Unless you know in advance (or specify) that your originals are to be separated by camera techniques, it is best to assume that a scanner will be used and, where you are able to influence this, provide your artwork in a suitable form, which in the case of a drum scanner means that it has to be flexible since it needs to be bent around the drum. This is unnecessary when a flat-bed scanner is involved although there could be limitations on the size of the board and its thickness, depending on the model used.

Colour originals

Colour line originals (normally reflection copy)

If it is to be reproduced by a camera, colour line artwork is best supplied as baseboard artwork drawn in black, with overlays to show each further colour likewise drawn in black, and all overlays registered to the baseboard artwork and to each other with register target marks.

An alternative is to draw the working for each colour which is easily separable from the others used (black-blue-orange, etc.). However, hand retouching at negative stage is normally still necessary, so this option is generally less preferable.

Coloured tone originals (reflection or transmission copy)

Coloured flat artwork (reflection copy)

Bear in mind these points:

☐ avoid fluorescent paints, which will not reproduce satisfactorily using process colours

☐ remember that certain very pure colours – purples, greens, mauves – will not be reproduced completely faithfully because of the limitations of the four-colour printing process

☐ ideally, present finished artwork somewhere between same-size and half-up

☐ if a drum scanner is to be used, ideally, present artwork on smooth surfaced, white board which can be stripped and wrapped round the drum (see above).

Colour prints (reflection copy)

There are three sorts:

☐ *dye-transfer* prints (made by a gelatine dye transfer principle)

☐ *negative-positive* colour prints (the standard 'en' print is of this sort)

☐ *Cibachrome* prints which are made from colour transparencies.

Dye-transfer and Cibachrome prints are less common and more expensive to make than conventional colour prints but accept hand retouching (with specific dyes) particularly well, and are often specified where extensive colour retouching is necessary to a subject.

Negative-positive colour prints are quite satisfactory, but accept hand retouching with difficulty. If in doubt over the reproduction quality of a retouched print, have a further colour print duplicate made and reproduce from this (if satisfactory) rather than the retouched print.

Bear in mind:

☐ aim for a print size s/s or larger than the size you need for the printed article

☐ glossy finish rather than matt, and certainly not embossed finish

☐ check that an anti-fade medium has not been used. Anti-fade media fluoresce badly in the camera and make separation difficult.

Colour transparencies (transmission copy)

Also known as *colour-reversal* films.
 Bear in mind these points:

☐ be sure to choose your transparencies on a light box with standard transmission lighting conditions as governed by BS950 Part 2. This will show you how the transparency should look when printed (with allowance for a loss in brightness – see below). Expect a very different result from that obtained by holding the transparency up to an electric light or up to a window

☐ transparencies normally have to undergo considerable enlargement, so contain this to the smallest factor you can by specifying a large transparency where you can (60 x 60 mm or similar from 120 roll film, rather than 24 x 36 mm size from a 35 mm camera)

☐ check carefully for evidence of focus faults or of chromatic aberration (out-of-register effect at the edges). Such faults will be greatly magnified with enlargement.

Sizing of illustrations

Reflection copy may be specifed for reproduction size either by outlining the area to be used, with the required finished dimensions marked, on a tissue overlay over the original; or if, like a bromide print, the original is translucent, by using a light box and marking the area required with its finished dimensions on the reverse in pencil. Be positive about size marking: clearly indicate with either a specific size, between definitive given points, or a percentage size, but this should always be the size to which the image is being made, NOT the amount by which the image is being reduced (e.g. 'reduce to 80%' NOT 'reduce by 20%').

If bleed is required it should be indicated and stated whether the size 'includes bleed' or is 'plus bleed'.

In either case, be careful not to damage the original by leaving pencil impressions on its surface.

Transmission copy – transparency material – is normally best dealt with by drawing an enlarged trace to the area required using a Grant projector or similar; or alternatively by masking off a black and white photoprint enlarged to the final size to show the dimensions and area required.

Simple scaling

A practical and simple method of sizing illustrations is the diagonal method (see diagram). On an overlay, or on the reverse side of a photograph, draw the upright AB of the area required. Next draw a rectangle of the finished size of your reproduction in the corner ADEF and rule a diagonal starting at A through E and onto the edge of the copy.

Any point along the diagonal if extrapolated to the left horizontally and vertically downwards, until they meet the edge and base line, gives an area of the original which would reduce to the required dimensions.

Alternatively this method can be used to find a depth from a known area and width. Simply rule round the area required (see bottom diagram) and draw a diagonal, then rule horizontal line G-H at the point where the distance from the left vertical to the diagonal is equal to the required width. It will then be found that the distance from H to the base is the height the image will reduce to.

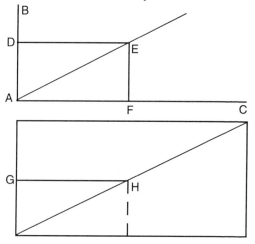

If you are unfamiliar with sizing illustrations, you may find it helpful to follow these steps.

1. Determine the general proportions required in the printed result (square, rectangle etc.). Then, bearing in mind these general proportions, determine the approximate area of the original that you want to display. Mask out any areas of the original that you know from the outset that you have to delete.

2. Ascertain the exact size of one dimension at which you need the printed illustration to appear. If working to a grid, for example, this might be the width of a one-column measure in a magazine; or the type measure in a book; or a predetermined width of box in a sequence of boxed illustrations.

3. Returning to the original, examine this same dimension (say, width) and measure the width of original which represents the contents you want to appear in the printed result. Mark this width (as two vertical lines) on either an overlay over the original, or on the back of the original.

4. If the dimension in para (2) is x mm and the dimension in para (3) is y mm, then x divided by y is the reduction factor being proposed (it might be 80% or 93% or etc.). Note this.

5. Look now at the depth of illustration required in the finished result. If the depth of the printed result is already determined by the requirements of layout, follow step 5a. If the depth of the printed result is flexible, follow step 5b.

a. Say the reduction in (4) is 80%. Then the depth of the original which you are allowed in order to arrive at your correct finished version will be 100 divided by 80 multiplied by your fixed depth of finished version. Calculate what this is, and mask off the original in its depth accordingly.

If this masking would delete an important part of the picture, you must either compromise and change this 'fixed' depth, adjusting other elements of the layout accordingly; or start again at para (3) with a different definition of the width dimension by masking more or less than you did before. This will achieve a different reduction factor and, with trial and error, will lead you to an acceptable result in the depth allowance of the original.

b. Say the reduction in (4) is 80%. Then turn to the original, choose your ideal depth of subject and mask this off. Then this depth of original x 80% gives the depth of the finished picture which will result. Scale and proportion can also be calculated using slide rules, scaling discs or simple scientific calculators.

Presentation of soft copy originals

Just as the pre-press production, having become more and more digital, can be moved nearer the document originator, the same is happening with images.

Digital images can be created in a number of ways

☐ on a personal computer/dtp system
☐ with a digital camera
☐ by using Kodak Photo CD

Personal computer/dtp system

There are numerous off-the-shelf design software packages available, one or more of which can be used to create a digital image. They will also normally provide the digital data in one of the commonly used formats so that it can be integrated in other application programs.

For example, there is TIFF (Tagged Image File Format), a contone image file description format for storing various resolutions, grey scales and colours.

Another format is Encapsulated PostScript (EPS) which is used for storing vector or object orientated artwork as well as bit maps. Thirdly, there is PICT, the format in which most Macintosh illustrations are encoded.

However, it needs to be recognised that some programs save TIFF images with subtle variations which might cause difficulties when they are being handled by other software, while it is normally not possible to alter an EPS file's contents without opening the file in its originating program, though it may be scaled, cropped and rotated.

Digital camera

Originally developed for newspaper photo journalists, uses for the digital camera are widening as the technology develops. Basically, it consists of a conventional unmodified professional camera with standard lenses and shutter mechanism but whose back has been replaced by a scanning device which transforms optical images into electronic signals.

Advantages include the ability to capture static and moving images, both 2D and 3D. The data can be saved on disk, or imported directly into image manipulation and hence page make-up programs.

Photo CD

Developed by Kodak, it enables 35 mm transparencies and larger film images to be scanned and written on to compact discs by a commercial film laboratory or graphics bureau: up to a hundred 35 mm film images can be stored on a single compact disc. These can then be played back on a video or television screen, be stored and retrieved digitally, or imported into a personal computer equipped with a CD-ROM disc drive for manipulation and pre-press applications.

Monochrome reproduction

Line reproduction

A modern process camera can reproduce images within a range from about 12% reduction to 1000% enlargement and, providing that the original has been correctly prepared and the appropriate exposure and film processing observed, correct images will be produced. With computerised cameras, after the initial programming, the computer controls exposures and, as most processing is carried out by machine, a high degree of consistency is achieved at the film negative stage of the printing process.

Line negatives on film

Three types of film are now in general use in the graphic reproduction departments and they are *lith*, *rapid access* and *third generation*. Lith is the premier reproduction film for line and half-tone work as it yields an image of ultrahigh contrast with no grey intermediate tones or soft edges. It has a fine grain and can be developed to high densities but is slower to use than some others.

Rapid access materials are conventional materials which are capable of being processed through developer, fixing and washing in a short time. This is achieved by using specially formulated chemistry and a high temperature. These materials used to suffer from the problem of having slightly soft edges to all lines and dots but the latest range of emulsions on the market produces images which very closely resemble the sharpness of lith reproductions. The only slight disadvantage is that the grain structure is large and they do not always develop to quite the same high densities as premium lith, but they are considerably quicker.

The third generation or hybrid films, as they are sometimes called, were developed, as the name implies, to take advantage of the main benefits of the other two film types, that is the speed and ease of use of rapid access plus lith-like quality. In fact, the latest versions have proved so successful that they are rapidly taking the place of lith.

Line photoprints on paper

Two sorts can be specified:

Negative and print

A negative film is made from the original, and the negative image is contact printed on photographic paper. It is possible to retouch the negative and then many prints can be made from it but the results can have slightly soft edges owing to the contrast of the paper.

Diffusion transfer or PMT (photomechanical transfer)

An original is exposed on to a special negative through the camera or contact exposure device; this negative is then fed into a special processor which activates the inbuilt developing agent in the material and then laminates it to a receiving sheet of either paper or film. After a short time the two sheets are peeled apart and a very sharp image is revealed. Paper prints produced in this way can be used in design studios for paste-up work, and film positives can be used for platemaking purposes. With the use of screens it is also possible to produce half-tone images by this method. The range of materials available now in diffusion transfer is extensive and by using different negative materials it is possible to obtain laterally reversed images, black to white reversals, continuous tone copies and even colour separations on panchromatic sensitive materials. The main disadvantages are single images from a negative and no facility for negative retouching.

Tone reproduction

Tone work can be processed through the camera, but increasingly is being scanned and incorporated with text matter in page make-up operations. All continuous-tone originals have to be broken down into half-tone dot formation in order to create the illusion of continuous tone when printed in one colour and weight of ink. The screen formation is normally laid at 45° to the base of the image as this is the angle which is least visible to the eye.

The type of screen formation can vary. The traditional *crossline screen* gives a square dot in the mid-tones rather like a chess board and in the printing process 'dot gain' occurs in these joined up dots which tends to increase the darkness of these tones, whilst the next tone lighter, which was not joined, does not increase to the same extent. Therefore a jump in tone density occurs, causing problems in smooth vignettes and flesh tones. To overcome these problems an *elliptical dot screen* was made which has 'kite shaped' or elliptical dots that join in one direction, then in a much darker tone join in the second direction giving a much smoother gradation.

Apart from the dot screens there is a range known as 'special effect screens' and these reproduce the tones in differing ways such as straight lines, wavy lines, concentric circles, linen, muslin and grain texture, brick effect and many others which may be selected to suit the aesthetic quality of the image.

The next variable that must be considered in tone reproduction is the fineness of the screen ruling, or the number of dots to the inch/cm. This will vary according to the printing process being used and the type of surface being printed on.

Half-tone negatives

The films used to produce half-tone negatives and positives are lith, third generation or rapid access. If reproduction is carried out on vertical darkroom cameras, the procedure would be to calculate the percentage enlargement or reduction required, then read the densities of the highlight and shadow areas of the copy. From this information exposures would be either calculated by the camera operator or, if a computerized camera were being used, the figures would be put into the computer which would calculate the necessary exposures and also make the allowances for size change.

The films would then be processed through the appropriate automatic film processor. If positives are required these would be made by simply contacting the negatives onto either a special 'contact' film or the same type as used to make the negatives.

Screen rulings

The following table may be used as a very rough guide for letterpress and litho. Figures are different again for the other processes and it is wise to consult the printer for a final decision.

lines per inch	lines per cm	paper surface	printing process
55–65	25/26	Newsprint	Letterpress
100	40	M.F.	Letterpress
120	48	Matt coated	Letterpress
133	54	Matt coated/Art	Letterpress
150	60	Art	Letterpress
100/120	40/48	Newsprint	Offset litho
133	54	MF/Matt coated/Art	Offset litho
150 - 300	60 - 118	Matt coated/Art	Offset litho

Half-tones on diffusion transfer materials

When individual pages are assembled mechanically using type which has been set on photographic paper, to be able to put the illustrations in place, line and half-tone prints are required to the correct size. All this illustration matter can be produced on diffusion transfer materials very efficiently. The system would be to bring the illustrations to the required size on the repro camera and expose them on to diffusion transfer paper which will produce good quality line and half-tone images as previously described. These are then pasted down in position and one negative made of the complete page. One thing that has to be considered is that every time an image is copied it increases slightly in contrast; therefore the prints that are made should be slightly lacking in contrast, i.e. highlight dots too large and shadows too open, so that when reproduced the final image on paper will be as required. The screen ruling used for these half-tone prints should never exceed 120/48 and indeed a coarser screen such as 100/40 or 110/44 should be considered.

Half-tone from printed copy

If already screened originals are reproduced an inferior result will always result mainly because the new half-tone will clash with the existing screen dots and moiré patterning will result to some degree. Recommended methods of reproduction are:

Dot for dot reproduction

Where the half-tone dots are dense black and sharp, with little change in the size and the screen ruling does not exceed 120/48 the illustration can be treated as a line copy, but a loss of highlight and shadow detail will occur giving a result greatly increased in contrast.

Diffusion technique

When dot for dot reproduction is not a possibility for any of the reasons stated above the image is made slightly out of focus and the screen ruling rotated 30° away from the existing screen ruling. This would minimize the moiré patterning. If a better quality image is required this can be achieved by having a copy print made photographically which can then be retouched and airbrushed before reproduction is carried out.

Duotone reproduction

In normal duotone reproduction, two half-tone shots of the original are taken at different screen angles and with different tonal ranges. The 'basic' shot at 45° is used to make the black plate, and the second shot at 15° is used to make a plate to be printed in a second colour. The effect is to introduce a rich, tonal effect to the original which extends its range and at the same time put a coloured 'tint' into the illustration.

Duotone reproduction for printing in two blacks, or in a black and a grey, should be considered as an option where the original bromide prints to be reproduced are particularly demanding, either in tonal range or in contrast, and the best possible quality of reproduction is required. In this case, the main print will be shot to give good highlight and middle-tone contrast, while the subsidiary print will add shadow contrast and detail. In this way the total density range reproduced can be considerably extended. See also the box on *Checking black half-tones*.

Screenless reproduction

For exceptional requirements 'screenless' litho reproduction and printing is a possibility, but it is offered by very few suppliers.

Although termed screenless the principle involved is in fact that of printing off the grain of the plate. Continuous-tone positives are made from the originals, and they are contact-printed to plates with a specially fine surface coating. Thereafter offset printing proceeds in much the normal way.

Everything depends on the quality of the platemaking – where tolerances are extremely fine – and on the quality of the plates themselves. Since no screen formation is visible, the rendering of detail possible is in theory very fine indeed.

Checking black half-tones

If a half-tone looks unsatisfactory in proof or in print, check the following:

☐ What was the quality of the original? A grey original will produce a grey print. At the other extreme, an original with a greatly extended tonal range or density cannot be reproduced entirely faithfully in mono black because of the limits of the printing process: whereas, for example, an average density range obtainable in printing black ink on white coated paper stops at around 1.6, a bromide print can reach a density range of 2.4 or beyond. Only a black/grey duotone printing will give an improved reproduction.

☐ Has the correct screen ruling been used for the kind of paper being printed? Check filling in.

☐ Is the detail generally muddy? Check the absorbency of the paper and the weight of ink carried (by an assessment of the typematter inking, for example). Either the absorbency of the paper or over-inking might have led to excessive dot gain (i.e. the half-tone dots have printed larger than they should). This could indicate a lack of quality control during printing, or a platemaking fault.

☐ If all the above can be eliminated, the fault is very likely in the origination itself. Check what densitometry controls (if any) were applied, and whether a single-shot or batched-up procedure was adopted. If doubt remains, a small printing plate made from one of the original illustration films used for the print run, and printed on a small machine with varied weights of ink, will normally reveal how far printing or original repro was to blame.

Desktop scanning

Within the last few years a range of desktop scanners has been available to enable graphics to be scanned into documents for business/office use or, at the higher end of the range, for graphic arts applications.

Most scanners have a *flat-bed* configuration (as distinct from the *drum* scanners mentioned elsewhere) so the artwork to be scanned is positioned on a sheet of glass under which a beam of light passes across the image to digitize the graphic as a series of black and white dots or pixels.

Some scanners have fixed resolution and, in this case, 300 dots per inch (dpi) is a common standard enabling the scanned resolution to match the typical output resolution of a laser printer attached to a desktop publishing system.

Other scanners have a choice of resolution level, which can be up to 1,000 dpi or more.

The output resolution is, however, determined by the output device, so a 600 dpi scan cannot be output by a 300 dpi printer at the higher resolution. Equally, a 300 dpi scan will be output by a 600 dpi printer at 300 dots, not 600.

The other principal quality condition attaching to desktop scanners is the number of grey scales which can be distinguished. 16 levels of grey is common, while an increasing number of devices distinguish 256 levels.

Scanning software which controls the operation of the machine and generates a screen image for editing or incorporating in a page make-up program frequently includes facilities which enable the image to be manipulated: at its most basic level, 'cleaned up' to delete extraneous dots picked up during the scanning and at its most sophisticated it can provide a number of graphics tools which facilitate re-drawing and effect creation.

Initially, problems involved in desktop scanning included relatively slow speed and the significant amount of storage needed for complex images. However, these have now been mainly overcome although it should be noted that the eventual reproduction is determined by the quality of output device and, in particular, by the resolution available to reproduce grey levels. As a general rule of thumb, resolutions below 2000 dpi cannot satisfactorily reproduce half-tones at 120 screen.

Despite a few limitations, desktop scanners have rapidly come into use in DTP systems where graphics have to be incorporated in pages and the quality, speed and sophistication of these machines have improved significantly.

Colour reproduction

Substantial economies can be made when originating and printing subjects in multi-colour line by ensuring that artwork is presented in the easiest way for separation.

In the case of the baseboard artwork fitted with registered overlays, no extra work is needed at the process camera stage provided that the overlays are registered accurately. Each overlay is removed in turn, shot separately on camera, and then joined up in register at imposition/plate-making stage.

In the case of colour line for camera separation, each colour is separated from the others by the use of filters in the camera. The principle involved is the same as that of process colour separation in that a filter of the same colour as one of the colour lines will transmit that colour and block all others. Each coloured line, when shot through a filter of its own colour, will therefore 'disappear' on the resulting negative, revealing the positions of the other lines sequentially. Therefore thought must be given to the colours of tri-colour filters when preparing the artwork (see *Theory of process colour separation*).

Filtration is seldom 100% effective in isolating the different elements of an original, and some retouching on the negatives is almost always necessary; so where the form of the original artwork can be influenced this method is much less to be preferred.

A number of colour reference schemes from Coates Lorilleux, Pantone, etc., are in universal use for specifying particular shades required. Probably the most comprehensive and widely used is the Pantone Matching System (PMS). Colour swatches are provided for over five hundred colour shades (with ink mixing formulae needed to arrive at each), with a range of the percentage tints corresponding to each solid shown as well.

The Pantone shade range is achieved from eight basic colours, together with transparent white and black. The eight basic shades are:

yellow
warm red
rubine red

Colour line reproduction

rhodamine red
purple
reflex blue
process blue
green

Where a solid area is marked for printing in a particular Pantone shade, and the job being printed uses process colours, it is normally acceptable – and certainly very much cheaper – to match the shade required using a combination of tints of the process colours instead of going to the expense of a further colour working.

For this purpose, the Pantone Corporation – and many of the larger origination houses – issue very comprehensive tint charts which will illustrate all the combinations of tints of the process colours printed one over the other.

Where a company logo or 'house colour' is involved, however, it is important to check with the client first on whether such tint matching is satisfactory.

See also *Make-up, imposition and planning.*

In order to understand the working of colour separation and printing, it is useful to understand a little of the theory involved. Here is a reference note.

Colour tone reproduction

Theory of process colour separation

In order to understand the principles of colour separation it is necessary first to know a little about additive mixing of coloured light, which is very different from the mixing of pigments, and the two must not be confused.

In a darkened room, if three beams of light were projected simultaneously on to a white screen, i.e. red, green, and blue violet, and they were superimposed as shown in the illustration, we would have the three lights together in the centre, followed by the combination of two lights and then on the outside the individual lights with no mixing. It would show that when the three lights overlap in the centre white light would be formed; this is because these three lights represent all the colours of the visible spectrum and are known as *spectrum primary colours.*

If any one of these spectrum primary colours is missing then the other two, additively mixed, form what is termed a complementary colour. Reference to the illustration will show:

primary colour	*complementary*	*formed by*
Blue violet	Yellow	Red and green
Green	Magenta	Red and blue violet
Red	Cyan	Green and blue violet

It may well be asked 'Why do colours appear as they are?' 'Why is grass green or a daffodil yellow?' The reason for this is that the pigmentation in grass absorbs the blue and red out of the spectrum; therefore green is the only colour to reflect and the daffodil absorbs the blue out of the spectrum so red and green are reflected and, as we have shown in the illustration, red and green light additively mixed make yellow.

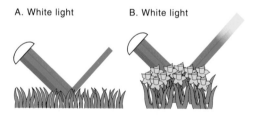

The diagram shows white light, which consists of red, green and blue, being projected at a green surface (a) and a yellow surface (b).

The colours we use in colour printing are yellow, magenta and cyan and since we have established that they are each made up from two primary colours, the following diagram will show how colour separation occurs. The filters used for this purpose are red, green and blue violet which are the spectrum primary colours and will only transmit their own colour.

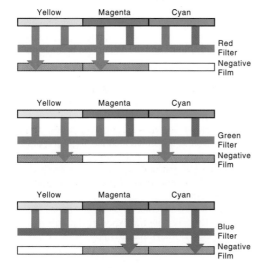

In the illustration the red filter transmits only light that comes from the yellow areas (since yellow = red and green) and the magenta areas (since magenta = red and blue violet). It is the red light transmitted from the coloured areas which produces the density on the separation negative.

Light coming from the cyan areas has no red reflection; therefore no density would record on the negative. In the same way if we consider the magenta separation for which the green filter is used:

the yellow and cyan areas have green reflections so therefore these would record no negative but the magenta which only has red and blue violet reflections would make no record. In a similar way the yellow separation negative, which is made through the blue filter, would record the blue reflections of the magenta and cyan but as no blue is present in yellow no image would record on the negative.

From these resulting negatives, positives would be made which, as they are the reverse of the negative, would have density wherever there was no image on the negative. Following the process through, the printing plates would be made and inked up in their appropriate colours of yellow, magenta and cyan. This explanation is, of course, for solid colours and the negatives are made on lith or third generation high contrast film, but if tones were introduced a continuous tone film, similar to that used in photography, would be used which would record the differing tones which go to make up the many colours required.

In four colour printing the black colour separation is used to add detail to the stronger colours and it is made in a variety of ways depending on the colours of the particular copy. The first method is to use a yellow or *gamma* filter which will lighten all yellows, oranges, reds and greens but does not clear out dark blue and mauve tones. The most efficient way is to make a partial exposure through all three of the colour filters in turn. In this way the proportions of exposure can be varied to suit the predominant colours of the copy and if any colour were absent then that colour filter would not be used.

After colour separation and colour correction has been carried out printing plates are then made and inked in the correct colours of yellow, magenta and cyan. When these are then printed in sequence and in register the coloured image is reproduced.

Procedures

Colour tone subjects can be separated by either a camera or electronic scanner. The vast majority of separation work is now done by scanning.

The following illustrations show a half-tone picture separated into its process colours.

The yellow separation.

The magenta separation.

The cyan separation.

The black separation.

The final four-colour picture.

Camera separations

Camera separations can be carried out using the three colour filters and continuous tone film as previously mentioned but this process produces only continuous tone negatives. These must then be converted into half-tone using a screen. With colour separations made by this method it is necessary to carry out extensive colour correction to compensate for the impurities in printing ink colours. This can be done either at the negative stage by making colour correction masks or on the final screen positive by hand retouching, or a combination of both methods.

The angles at which the screens are laid for the various colours are usually 45°, 75°, 105° and 90°

Scanner correction

Modern colour scanners can correct many of the faults listed below but an extra charge could possibly be incurred.

Overall colour cast A subject photographed against a stongly coloured background may have acquired a colour cast of the same shade. An overall colour bias may have been introduced during processing. In either case, the best solution is to have a duplicate transparency made with the fault corrected.

Marks Beware fingermarks, scratches, small blemishes etc., all of which will become very obvious when the transparency is enlarged.

Grain Unless graininess is a required effect, beware the result of excess enlargement with (typically) a 35mm transparency shot on fast film (ASA 400 or above).

Exposure An over-exposed original will reproduce with burnt out highlights and a generally weak rendering of colour. An under-exposed original will reproduce with muddy and ill defined colours, which will be worst in the shadows. The ideal density range should be within 0.4 at highlights and 2.5 at shadows. Beyond these points detail will not reproduce adequately.

Emulsion Ensure that the transparency is correct reading. The reproduction house will always assume that the image is right reading when the transparency is viewed with the emulsion away from you. If this is not the case, as with duplicates, supply a tracing or print showing how the image is to appear.

Consistency If you are considering page-planning transparencies together for scanning, check the consistency of their colour ranges and densities, and adjust by having duplicates made where necessary.

and it is normal to find the yellow on 90° but the other three colours are changed by various companies. The rule is that the main colours must be exactly 30° away from each other to avoid moiré patterning.

Scanning

Scanners work by scanning the original coloured artwork in a series of lines. In the case of drum scanners, the original is wrapped round the scanning drum and if transparent copy a beam of light would be projected from the centre of the drum through the copy into a lens system. This beam would then pass through a beam splitter and the separate beam for

Manipulating images with a scanner

A scanner will normally produce an image which is a 'facsimile' of the original copy but it is also possible to manipulate the image in various ways, some of which are as follows:

Distortion: instead of enlarging or reducing to the same degree in height and width, separate factors may be entered for each direction.

Colour casts: if the original has a cast in any particular colour this can be removed as an overall correction but it means that all of that particular colour would be changed.

Pastel boost: when colours are pale, such as in over-exposed transparencies or wash-drawings, extra density may be added to any or all three colours, but not 'spot' colour.

Unsharp masking: if this control is used it has the effect of putting a 'halo' around all detail, making it appear sharper in reproduction.

Catch lights: are used completely to drop-out all the dots in the highlight areas, used in the reproduction of cut-glass, silverware etc.

Lateral reversal: will produce an image which is reversed left to right compared with the copy.

Tonal gradation: can be used to accentuate either the details in the highlight or shadow areas of the original without distorting the colour balance.

Undercolour removal and polychromatic colour reversal are techniques for limiting the amount of ink used in printing.

each of the three colours would go into the photo multipliers and computers where the colour correction and manipulation is controlled. In the case of reflection copy, this is mounted on an opaque drum and a reflection light shone on to it. This in turn is picked up by the lens system and onwards in the same way as in transmission copy.

When the colours have been manipulated they can be exposed on to film in either negative or positive form on the output side of the scanner. On modern machines this is done using a laser which generates a dot formation that can be modified to give various screen rulings and dot shapes. The range of reproduction size available varies but is generally from 20% to 2500% and a modern scanner will expose approximately 60mm plus of film per minute. This can be one, two or four colours at a time depending on the size of the reproduction and the size of the scanner.

The alternative to a drum scanner is a flatbed device. This reads originals held flat normally like a photocopier. Instead of lasers and photo multipliers, most use ccd (charged coupled device) sensors which turn the information from the reflected original into electrical signals.

The ccds are normally in a linear array which covers the width of the image area and travels the length of the bed. The number of ccds determines the scanning resolution. As the technology has advanced and ccds have become smaller so a greater number of them can be put into an array.

Consequently, although originally most flatbed scanners were considered only suitable for lower quality work, this need not be the case any more. Indeed, the differences between them and drum scanners has blurred considerably although flat-bed scanners still have the advantage of not having to wrap the original around the drum. On the other hand, they tend to be mainly used for reflection originals though many models can also handle transparencies.

Electronic correction and page make-up systems

A significant advantage of scanning over traditional camera separation is that all the colour information is held in digital form in a computer. This allows the images to be manipulated and imported into page make-up systems, as does the scanning of monochrome halftones.

Originally, this required proprietary systems such as Linotype-Hell's Chromacom, Crosfield's Studio 800, Dainippon Screen's Sigmagraph and Scitex's Response which enabled a wide range of colour correction, retouching and image assembly functions to be performed on a video screen before final separated films were produced on a scanner.

Typical steps might have been:

☐ the original/originals were scanned as described above but instead of being output directly to film, the digital image was passed into the system as was the text matter.

☐ sitting at a workstation, the operator would then perform a variety of functions including colour correction of each individual colour subject, retouching, ruling, stripping in headlines, etc., and finally bring it all together with the typematter as a composed page.

The colour console includes:

☐ a stylus and digitizing tablet (for pointing at and outlining areas on the screen)
☐ a set of four sliding colour bars (for colour mixing)
☐ a thumb wheel (for colour correction adjustments)
☐ a viewing box (for composing an original with its separated image on screen).

Such systems required vast amounts of computing power and information storage, and were correspondingly expensive. As such they were generally only found in the larger companies and reproduction trade houses.

However, since then computer power and storage media has significantly dropped in price. For example, a PowerPC personal computer has more power than one of the original proprietary workstations but the cost is less than one hundredth.

Initially, the proprietary system suppliers took advantage of these developments by using this standard platform hardware as part of its systems. Off-the-shelf packages were becoming increasingly sophisticated. In order to bring prices down the manufacturers started using standard platform hardware.

Desktop colour systems

A typical example was Scitex's IPSO-1, a complete PostScript colour system which comprised an input scanner and output imagesetter with a Macintosh controlling the operations. Because the system was based on a Macintosh, it could run off-the-shelf colour manipulation packages such as PhotoShop and ColourStudio.

Eventually, the stage was reached where proprietary hardware was virtually completely replaced by standard platform workstations and proprietary software now tends to be used just for specialist applications, as it became recognised that dtp image manipulation software packages particularly Abode's Photoshop as well as the dtp page make-up programs can provide everything necessary for producing general commercial work.

Proofing

Black and white methods

It is normally sufficient to see proofs of black and white illustrated work in photocopied, digitally printed or the more traditional diazo, ozalid or blueprint form.

Where there are specific reasons for needing to see the printed quality of black half-tones, however, it may be appropriate to see machine proofs. In such cases the illustrations may be proofed either in random order – *scatter proofing* – or else imposed in final position. Where there are large numbers of dark half-tones, or solids, then imposed machine proofs – with the illustrations in the same track as they will be when they are finally printed – will be the safer option.

Colour methods

Colour work can be proofed in numerous ways depending on the accuracy of the final result that is required and the budget available. Some of the simpler systems were designed only to check impositions but the more elaborate ways are obviously closer to the printed result and experience will show the amount of variation you can expect and judgement can be made on this basis.

There are four main types of proofs:
- photographic
- photomechanical laminates
- wet
- digital

Photographic

Mainly used for checking content, positioning and register, these systems tend to be simple and economical to produce. However, they do vary in their technology which ranges from diffusion transfer to overlay films which are exposed to each colour separation negative or positive and then processed. Thus the proof consists of separate layers of film, the number depending on the number of colours being used.

Photomechanical laminates

Again systems vary somewhat, but basically they consists of dry toners and light sensitive adhesive polymer sheets or light sensitive coloured sheets. These are exposed to each separated negative or positive film in turn and after processing develop an image in the corresponding colour. The sheets are then built up on top of each other, laminated together and transferred on to a special base.

Experience is needed in assessing such proofs properly but, given this experience, they can prove an excellent and reliable method of checking reproduction, especially now that they can for example simulate dot gain and different printing stocks or even in some cases be transferred on to the printing stock itself.

Wet proofing

Four proofing plates are made, and the job is proofed on a flatbed proofing press or, if feasible, on the production machine to be used. This is certainly the best method to achieve a realistic proof of what the job should look like when printed, but to ensure that the production run can match the proof, check through the following:

☐ ensure that a complete set of colour bars are run with the proof. These will give a comprehensive and accurate read-out of any faults, as well as giving information on density levels, dot gain, trapping, grey balances, etc., which can be compared by the printer with the values being recorded while the job is being printed.

☐ ensure that a good set of progressives is made in the order of colours in which the printer will want to print. Obtain this sequence from the printer: many alternative schemes are used, and all are equally valid.

☐ the same paper is being used for proofing as for final printing. A proof pulled on gloss art on a flatbed proofing press will (for example) show much less dot gain – and hence appear much sharper – than it will be feasible to expect on a web run with cheap matt art or cartridge paper. Make an allowance for this discrepancy if production run paper is not available.

☐ ensure that standard inks BS 4666 specification, non intensified, are used.

☐ some printers give a data sheet detailing their method of working, printing sequence and machines, dot gain allowance under normal conditions, etc. Obtain this where it is available and so require the proofing house to follow the same procedures that will be followed at final printing stage.

Illustrations may be proofed either in random order, as scatter proofs, or in their final, imposed order. Where subjects are difficult and the quality requirement is high, imposed proofs with all the illustrations in the same track as they will be for the final printing, are the only safe option.

Digital proofing

As pre-press becomes more and more digital, such proofing systems are becoming increasingly popular. Like analogue proofing, there are a variety of technologies available depending on the quality of the result required and the budget.

Although originally considered less reliable than analogue proofs, particularly as the majority of systems produce continuous tone rather than simulate halftone, the technologies are advancing rapidly. They range from rip driven digital colour copiers with their relatively high hardware but low consumable costs to thermal dye sublimation printers where capital outlay is less but consumable costs are much more.

However, the quality of the proof is also higher and can be contract although they can be rather 'photographic' in appearance due to the white resin coated substrate which is imaged by heating four colour dyed ribbons (cmyk).

Then there is a range of ink-jet printers which at one end of the scale provide checking capabilities and at the other contract type although still continuous tone proofs. Normally with these systems liquid ink is sprayed through fine nozzles on to most paper stock. Thus the consumable costs tend to be on the low side, while the price of the equipment depends on the quality of proof being produced.

At the very top of the range both in terms of proof quality and cost are the electrophotographic and dry laser systems. However, they can provide halftone contract quality proofs to printer's specification of stock, ink densities and dot gain.

When marking proofs for correction, be very careful about making specific technical instructions to alter colours in a certain way – 'take down magenta', 'less cyan here', etc. – unless you know exactly what you are doing and are able to foresee how this instruction will affect the other colours around it. There are normally several ways technically to get to the same desired end result: the best instruction is therefore to say what you want – 'less orange here', 'not so purple here', etc., by reference to the original – and leave it to the technician or retoucher to obtain the effect in the most appropriate way.

A system of colour proof correction marks has been published – BS4785:1972 – although it is not often used. It may however help you in codifying the sort of instructions it might be useful to make, even if the exact symbol itself is not used:

Colour correction marks

No	Instruction	Symbol	Notes
1	Increase contrast.		
2	Reduce contrast.		
3	Correct outline.		
4	Increase detail.		
5	Decrease detail.		
6	Delete part of copy.		Strike through are to be deleted.
7	Move to . . .		Indicate the distance of the move and ring the area affected.
8	Change colour to . . .		Ring area affected and annotate 'See colour sample supplied' or 'Change to specified colour', etc.
9	Change black to white or white to black.		
10	Alter to size indicated.		Reference should be made to a layout for repositioning.
11	Mirror change lateral reversal.		
12	Exchange position.		Circled those areas to be exchanged.
13	Improve register.		
14	Attend to obvious fault.		Fault should be circled.
15	Invert image.		

Colour bars

Colour bars give the proofer, printer and quality controller vital information about both ink and press performance, and you should expect any critical colour job to be both proofed and run with standard colour bar controls. Some permit visual checks. Others need instrumentation checks.

A number of patent colour bar structures are available. The most common are:

☐ Gretag CMS colour bar
☐ GATF colour bar

☐ Hartmann colour bar
☐ Eurostandard Cromalin colour bar

Colour bars have all or most of the following components:

Printing down controls

A series of microlines (6–16 microns or thereabouts) and highlight dots (0.5% – 5% dot) which permit assessment of how accurately a plate has been printed down from film to plate.

Solid density patches

For each colour. Monitor solid density and therefore ink film thickness. These are read with a densitometer. Characteristic values should be (art paper):

Yellow	0.80 to 1.00
Cyan	1.20 to 1.40
Magenta	1.20 to 1.40
Black	1.40 to 1.60

Trapping patches

Trapping patches show one solid process colour printed on top of another in a number of combinations to establish how far each ink is being properly accepted in 'wet-on-wet' printing.

Screen patches (often 25% and 75%)

For each colour. Monitor dot gain, which if not correctly allowed can lead to very wide variations in the appearance of a half-tone. (Variables which contribute to dot gain are ink film thickness, ink viscosity, plates, blankets and press settings.) Characteristic values for art paper at 75% tone are between 8% and 14% gain.

Coarse and fine screen half-tone patches

For each colour. For inspection of half-tone formation and print, and additional assessment of dot gain (as above). A dot gain scale, incorporated into the GATF bar, allows a visual check by means of a scale, similar to a grey scale. This works on the principle that fine screen tints are more sensitive to dot gain than coarser tints. The scale is made up of 10 steps in 200 lines-to-the-inch screen ruling, in the form of numbers 0-9, against a background of a 65 lines-to-the-inch tint of uniform strength. Increasing amounts of dot gain show up as more of the numbers 0-9 become filled in and visible.

Slur gauge

Slur patches reveal directional dot gain caused by slurring or doubling. They are normally in the form of 'star targets' or slur oblongs, which indicate visually if a colour is being slurred or doubled.

Grey balance

Grey balance patches print a cyan 50%, magenta 40% and yellow 40% tint one on another which should if all is in balance yield a neutral grey. A purely visual check.

5 Make-up, imposition and planning

Make-up and imposition

Until relatively recently, make-up was generally a manual operation, often using text galleys produced on film or on paper, with line or half-tone film or paper for the illustrations or with illustrations also photoset.

In such instances, material could come from several sources:

☐ output from a photosetter can be either on positive or negative film or bromide paper
☐ typematter from a strike-on, or laser printing system on plain paper
☐ typematter from a hot metal composition system on special repro paper
☐ illustrations produced by camera or scanner on film or paper.

Film make-up materials

Film make-up is preferred where high-quality reproduction of text and half-tone images is required. Multicolour work is always made up in film.

Phototypesetting film consists of a high-speed, high-contrast emulsion supported on a polyester film base. The image formed on the film is conventionally identified according to its appearance when viewed from the emulsion side. Thus when viewing the film from its emulsion side, a *reverse reading* film has its image the wrong way round or reversed. Also called *wrong reading*. This type of film is used for lithographic platemaking.

A *right-reading* film contains an image which appears the right way round when viewed from the emulsion side. This type of film is used for direct printing methods such as letterpress.

All modern imagesetters can produce reverse or right-reading film in negative or positive format.

Materials

Films produced by camera or scanner for line or half-tone work are based on high contrast emulsions.

Paper make-up materials

Paper make-up is best used for text work which contains average quality illustrations in line or tone. The method is generally simpler to handle and proof than film make-up which is more difficult to judge visually and more expensive.

Phototypesetting paper

The main type of phototypesetting paper in use is resin coated paper (RC). This is a top quality paper with conventional high-speed, high-contrast emulsion specially formulated for high temperature processing.

An alternative, although not much used now, is stabilization paper. Of lower cost than RC paper, stabilization paper contains a developing agent in its emulsion which is activated and stabilized during processing. Processing is therefore rapid and requires a simple processor machine. Image stability on processed film and paper is adequate for rapid make-up work, but since the image can discolour with time it is not suitable for work which will stand for months before printing, or for repeat work.

Strike-on repro paper

Any smooth, white coated paper can yield a satisfactory typed image which will reproduce well for make-up purposes. All typing images should be produced using a one-time-carbon ribbon.

Hot metal repro paper

Traditionally, *Baryta* paper was used for hot metal reproduction, although a heavy, smooth art paper also yields satisfactory results.

Storing CRC

Do not rely on stabilization paper if CRC has to be stored for any length of time. The image will rapidly 'go off'. Wherever possible, keep electronic files in place of, or in addition to, photoset material.

Photographic print paper

Paper *photomechanical transfers – PMTs –* can be used for producing combined text and illustration make-up. The PMT produces a high-contrast image via an inexpensive and simple processing system.

Manual make-up in either film or paper is the process of assembling text and illustration elements to form pages or formats ready for printing.

Methods

Film make-up is preferred in the following circumstances:

☐ where half-tone illustrations of a screen ruling greater than 100 lines per inch are required
☐ where multicolour and close register images are required
☐ where high quality reproduction is required.

Paper make-up is preferred in the following circumstances:

☐ where the image is line work and half-tone screen ruling does not exceed 100 lines per inch
☐ where speed and flexibility in production are required
☐ where little registration is necessary (monochrome work)
☐ where multiple assembly of small elements, boxes and rules is required.

Film make-up methods

In the UK, although not for instance in Sweden nor the USA, film make-up is generally performed using positive film, it being felt that the dense background of negative films makes complex assembly more difficult. However, negative films may be used for simple work.

Make-up begins with the drawing of an accurate layout of the job on white paper, normally using a layout table and pre-printed grids. The layout indicates clearly the position of text, illustrations, rules and boxes, etc., and contains cutting guide marks, folding marks and any other information necessary to ensure a correct make-up in film. A clear carrier sheet of polyester or acetate is positioned over the

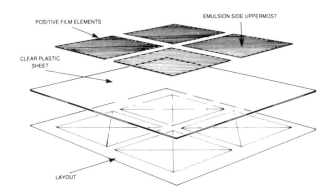

POSITIVE FILM ELEMENTS

EMULSION SIDE UPPERMOST

CLEAR PLASTIC
SHEET

LAYOUT

layout sheet and the film elements for the job are assembled, emulsion side uppermost, and affixed to the base sheet with adhesive or pressure-sensitive tape. Film is cut to size with a scalpel and arranged so that each separate element does not overlap its neighbour but is assembled to leave a uniform flat surface.

Note that the best results are obtained when the emulsion side of the film is able to make close contact with the sensitized plate coating at the platemaking stage. Multi-colour film make-up follows the same procedure as monochrome work, with a separate carrier sheet used for each colour. The registration between one colour element and another has to be meticulously observed, and this is achieved using a pin-register system.

A frequent requirement in making up colour assemblies is to lay tints for each of the four process colours in specified areas. Borders, boxes and panels are frequently produced in this way. A particular tint of colour is chosen by reference to a patent colour chart which shows how that tint may be achieved from process colour inks. For example, a tint of brown needed for a panel would require a 40% cyan tint, a 60% magenta tint and a 80% yellow tint. Tints of these values are therefore assembled to register on separate carrier sheets to obtain the required result.

Where the assembly of film elements, text, half-tones, tints, etc., is complex, the assembly can be contacted with a positive-working daylight film which will reproduce the entire assembly on one sheet of film called a *final*.

Single colour proofing

Film make-up assemblies can be proofed by *dyeline* or *diazo* process (contact ammonia prints), often called *blueprints* or *ozalids*. These prints on paper are normally in the same form as the assembly – positive film yielding a positive proof – although reversal diazo is also possible. Such proofs do not give a high quality result and their use is for checking image position and place of elements.

The normal image colours for dyeline proofs are dark blue, black or red.

Multi-colour proofing

Colour proofs are most commonly produced by plastic laminate methods since this is cheaper and faster than wet (press) proofing when small numbers are involved and avoids the expense of printing plates and machine time.

In the case of DuPont's Cromalin system, for example, each separation film in turn is exposed to its own special material which after processing develops an image in the colour corresponding to it. The layers of special material, one for each of the colours, are then built up on top of each other – laminated together – and provide a good visual image of the separation quality. There are a number of such systems available including Agfaproof and 3M's Matchprint which gives a similar quality of result although the chemical process is somewhat different.

Paper make-up methods

Paper make-up is performed by pasting the type, line and tone elements (all of which are produced on paper) on a base layout sheet. This base sheet has the element positions drawn in, or may be a pre-printed grid, with special blue lines.

Duplicating film

When films are duplicated or con-tacted during the production process, emulsion to emulsion contact is normally recommended. This process reverses the image, so that a reverse-reading positive, when contacted to film, emulsion to emul-sion, will yield a right-reading negative. Producing film duplicates may involve one of the following methods:

Using normal negative-working film

a reverse-reading positive

⇓

a right-reading negative (intermediate)

⇓

a reverse-reading positive (final)

Using positive-working film (autoreversal)

a reverse-reading positive

⇓

a reverse-reading positive (final)

All lith-type films used in reproduction are *orthochromatic*: that is, sensitive to the blue end of the light spectrum only. In practice this means that red records on film as does black, but blue does not record at all. Layout lines in blue on the base sheet therefore act as a guide to positioning elements without recording when the final assembly is photographed.

Line illustrations in paper make-up can be produced as PMT prints which are pasted in with text matter. Half- tone illustrations of no more than 100 lines per inch can be produced on bromide paper or PMT material and pasted in like line work. An alternative method is to cut a black or red mask corresponding to size and position of the illustration and place this with the text matter. When the make-up is photographed, the resulting negative film has clear windows in the masked area, and film half-tones are positioned in the windows. The final negative can be contacted to lithographic plate (negative working) or can be contacted to film to provide a final film positive of make-up.

Paper make-up is not suitable for multicolour work because of the difficulty of registration of images, and paper is not as dimensionally stable as film for close register work.

Proofing

Proofs from paper make-up can be produced by photocopying the finished assembly. Originally, this method did not produce a quality image but was used for checking the position of elements on the assembly and reading text. Also, the stripping lines of the make-up reproduced on the photocopy proof, although they were removed during the process of making press plates from the make-up. However, with modern photocopiers the image quality has improved tremendously and the stripping lines can be eliminated at this stage.

Storage

Paper make-up assemblies can be stored for long periods without detriment so long as the following precautions are followed:

☐ all paper elements - text from photosetter, bromide prints and PMTs - must be thoroughly washed after processing to remove all traces of chemical which will cause discolouration in time

☐ each make-up assembly should be protected with a cover sheet of paper

☐ storage should be in a location where temperatures are always steady and dry

☐ avoid use of all stabilization materials in make-up which is to be stored.

Imposition is the term used to describe the planning of magazine and book pages in such an ordered pattern that, when the printed sheet is folded, the page numbers run in correct sequence. The manner in which the printed sheet is folded is determined by the folding methods used in the finishing department, and it is this folding method which guides the planner. It is therefore essential for the planner to reach detailed agreement with the finishing department as to the type of imposition, place of lay edges, signature marks, collation marks, gutters and margins, etc. The nationally agreed standards in the UK are: *BPIF Folding Impositions Part 1. Imposition for book printing* and *BPIF Folding Impositions Part 2. Imposition schemes for trade finishers and general printing.* These can be obtained from the British Printing Industries Federation, 11 Bedford Row, London WC1R 4DX.

Basic principles of imposition

The folding of the sheet is the starting point of an imposition scheme. The illustration indicates the principles using a 16 page as an example.

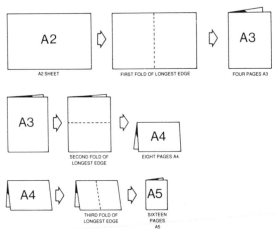

Terms in common use

Section A single printed sheet folded to final size, i.e. a 16 page section is made up of one printed sheet which contains 16 pages.

Collating Normally used for the gathering of sheets. However, strictly it is the checking system used to ensure sequential page numbers when sections are gathered together.

Signature Usually the name given to a printed sheet after it has been folded but is also the alphabetical letter or figure placed on the first page of each section to facilitate collating.

Sheetwork A printing method whereby pages are imposed in two forms, one printed on one side and the other on the reverse (backing up).

Work and Turn When matter is printed in its entirety on both sides of a sheet by using the same gripper edge.

Work and Tumble A printing method whereby the sheet is printed on one side and then turned over so that its gripper edge becomes the back edge of the sheet.

When planned as sheetwork the outer imposition is planned on one plate and the inner imposition on another plate. The printed sheet size of SRA 2 will form one 16 page section when folded:

7	10	11	9
2	15	14	3

Gripper

5	12	6	8
4	13	16	1

Gripper

When planned as work and turn the outer and inner impositions are placed together on one plate. The printed sheet size of SRA1 will produce two 16 page sections when cut and folded:

4	5	6	3
13	12	11	14
16	9	10	15
1	8	7	2

Gripper

Planning procedures

Film planning is the assembly of all the film elements required to make a single lithographic plate which will vary in size according to the size of the press. It is usual for paper make-up to be assembled two or four A4 size pages at a time and photographed. If a larger press is used, the resulting film is planned up with others to make a press plate which will carry eight, 16 or 32 pages. The press plate is made by exposing it to light through negative or positive film. With a simple image, a single element of negative or positive film is positioned on the plate and exposed in a printing-down frame. Where an image is more complex, and several film elements are assembled together for platemaking, these are planned up and supported by a base sheet of clear plastic called a planning *flat* or *foil*.

The position of images on the plate, the placing of pages, is determined by the way in which the final printed sheet is cut and folded. In bookwork the pages must be planned on the plate so that when cut and folded the book pages run in sequence. This whole process is governed by rules of imposition.

Planning for magazine, booklet or bookwork involves the highest degree of accuracy in positioning film elements so that when printed they back up correctly, print with constant margins and close register of multi-colour images.

Single colour planning

The most common form of single colour mechanical planning is the use of negative film elements assembled together on either paper (*goldenrod* or *poppy paper*) or clear plastic sheet (*foil*). The resulting assembly is called a *planning flat*.

Paper planning flats

Goldenrod paper of approximately $100g/m^2$ contains a colour dye which prevents UV radiation passing through it. When used for lithographic platemaking it prevents exposure of the plate to the UV light source and therefore acts as a mask. It is used as a base for planning single colour negatives. The layout is drawn onto the goldenrod paper and the negative film elements attached in position with pressure sensitive tape, emulsion side uppermost. Windows are then cut into the goldenrod paper to allow light to pass through the image areas. The assembled flat is then placed onto the press plate and exposed in the printing down frame; all non-image areas of the plate are protected from exposure by the goldenrod paper.

This method is not suitable for work which requires close registration because the goldenrod paper is not dimensionally stable.

Plastic planning flats

The plate layout indicating page positions, etc., is made on white paper and positioned beneath a sheet of clear plastic (acetate or polyester). The negative film elements are planned according to the layout and taped down or fixed with adhesive, emulsion side uppermost. When all film elements are fixed in position the flat is turned over and the non-image areas are covered with either goldenrod paper or masking strip film (a low tack red or amber coloured film membrane).

Multi-colour planning

The manual procedure for planning each individual flat of a multi-colour set is very similar to single colour planning using plastic flats. A layout showing the position of all film elements is drawn up on to white paper. The first base sheet of clear plastic is placed over the layout and the film elements corresponding to a single colour (normal selection being cyan or magenta). Since great accuracy and close register are required for multi-colour work, all multi-colour planning is done using positive film elements at least in the UK. Two methods of planning are used for close register work.

Pin register

This system utilizes a special punch to produce location holes in film and plate. Once a film element is punched it can be located and registered with another film element using register pins. Thus film produced in camera or scanner can be punched and registered accurately on location pins. Planning flats when punched can be correctly aligned with others using register pins. Planning flats so punched can be accurately located on the press plate at the platemaking stage on pins. Press plates which are punched can be quickly located on the press plate cylinder on pins in the plate clamps:

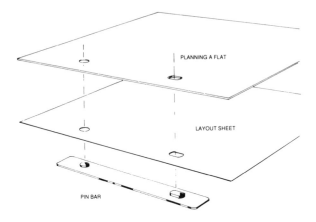

PLANNING A FLAT

LAYOUT SHEET

PIN BAR

Blue and red keys

With this method, a layout is drawn and the first planning flat assembled usually using the magenta or cyan film elements. The completed flat is then exposed in contact with a sheet of blue or red dyeline film and when processed produces a key image of the original flat in blue or red. In the case of blue line keys, each colour film element is registered in position using the blue to give accurate sighting. When complete the blue key planning flat is used for platemaking in the normal way; the blue image on the flat does not record on the final plate.

In the case of the red keys, the colour red will record on the press plate. Therefore it is used only as a colour guide to accurate register, much in the same way as a layout sheet. The red key is placed beneath a clear sheet of plastic and the film elements are assembled by using the red image as a register point.

Blue and red keys are often used in combination with pin register methods.

5

Machine planning

All the planning procedures discussed here can be computerized. One system utilizes a computer assisted camera which uses camera-ready copy, presented in predetermined order, and assembles these in correct sequence to produce a final negative ready for platemaking.

Another system photographs each camera-ready page onto 35mm or 70mm roll film and then sequences this to correct size to produce a negative for platemaking, or may be used to expose directly to the press plate.

It is also possible to plan the pages when they are still in digital form using dtp or special software thus enabling computer to plate operations. In other words, the plate is imaged directly from the page make-up workstation using a laser imagesetter (for polyester plates) or a special platesetter which is capable of handling metal plates.

Bookwork

Bookwork pages are planned using the following terminology:

Head This is the white space at the top of the page between the text and the trim. The normal imposition scheme brings the head of one page together with the head of another page. A trim allowance between the heads is normally 3mm for each page, thus an allowance for trim between heads is 6mm.

Foot This is the white space at the bottom of the page between the text and the trim.

Tail When an imposition scheme brings the foot of one page against the foot of another page the trim margin of 6mm between them is called the tails.

Fore edge This is the white space on the outer edge of the paper between the text and the trim.

Gutters Where an imposition scheme brings the fore edge of one page against the fore edge of another page, the trim margin between them of 6mm is called the gutters.

Backs The white space between the text and the spine of the page. The backs have no trim.

6 Platemaking and printing

Lithography

All the trends in Prepress technology, including make-up, imposition and planning, are moving towards computerisation which can integrate the keyboard operation to produce text with the scanning of illustrations, page make-up, merging of text and tone, with a final output direct to the press plate which as in the case of Heidelberg's GTO-DI press, for example, can be already placed on the press's cylinder. However, the manual methods described here are expected to continue alongside computer development for the foreseeable future particularly due to the variety of originals involved in many jobs.

Conventional metal litho plates are produced by exposing the planning flat which is held in vacuum contact with a light sensitive plate. This operation is performed in a printing-down frame which has a glass framed compartment in which the press plate and planning flat are held in close contact by vacuum pressure, while being exposed to high energy, ultra-violet radiation.

On exposure to ultra-violet light the sensitized coating of a *negative-working* plate undergoes a photo-chemical change to form an image on the plate which will carry printing ink.

The unexposed plate coating is removed during processing and non-image areas of the surface are rendered water-attracting/ink rejecting. In the case of *positive-working* plates, the sensitized coating is made unstable on exposure to ultra-violet light and thus is easily removed on processing. This leaves the unexposed coating on the plate to form the ink attracting image.

Alternatively, paper or plastics plates can be used, particularly for lower runs (normally up to 50,000). These can be produced in a number of ways

Platemaking

including electrostatic and photo-mechanical-transfer methods as well as laser imaging and photographic.

Conventional platemaking

The imposition and planning of film elements to form a planning flat for printing down are considered in an earlier section. As explained, completed planning flats for platemaking will be either in positive or negative film format. In either case both positive and negative film will be *reverse reading*.

Negative-working metal plates

Traditionally, in the UK these plates are used for single colour printing from short to large print runs (to approximately 200,000 copies). The plates are supplied ready coated with a light-sensitive compound (photopolymer) and are referred to as *pre-sensitized* plates. Exposure and processing of this type of plate is within five minutes, using an automatic plate processor. Processing removes the unexposed coating (*development*) and applies a gum solution to the non-image areas of the plate to make it water-attracting/ink rejecting (*fixing*).

Positive-working metal plates

Since positive planning is normally used in the UK for multi-colour work, the positive-working press plate is used mainly for such work. Processing of this plate is similar to negative-working plates although development removes the exposed coating from the plate. Since positive planning techniques often require the exposure of overlay flats (tints and burn-out masks), the exposure and processing time for these plates may extend the exposure and processing time can be longer than that for negative plates.

Paper/plastics platemaking

Initially, these plates were used on small-offset presses in the A4/A3 sizes designed for short run printing (under 1000 copies). However, materials are now available which can handle runs up to 50,000. The plates can be imaged in a number of ways including by a laser printer or imagesetter, or a process camera. Other methods can include electrostatic systems which expose the plate via paste-up copy through a lens system, and the image is formed on the plate electrostatically and fixed by heat or solvent. Plates made by the PMT process are produced by exposing a negative paper material in direct contact with paste-up copy and then contacting this negative with the plate in a chemical solution. The image formed on the negative paper transfers to the plate to form a printing image.

Camera platemaking systems which produce plates off a reel by exposure to camera ready copy are also available.

Conventional litho plates

The majority of litho plates are made of aluminium sheet of varying thicknesses (between 0.5 and 1.0 mm) with a surface grain or granular finish. This grain serves to give water-carrying properties to the plate and to give anchorage to the image forming material. Practically all plates today are of the pre-sensitized type, supplied ready coated with a light sensitive diazo compound or photopolymer resin material.

Negative-working plates

The coating on these plates is changed on exposure to ultraviolet radiation; in the case of diazo compounds, light causes a chemical change in the crystal structure of the compound which renders it ink attracting. Diazo coated plates however have a shorter press life (up to 150,000 runs) than photopolymer coated plates although they are capable of runs up to 250,000 if prelacquered and are used for short run and small offset work. Photopolymer resin coatings were developed to give long press runs (250,000 plus copies). The polymer structure of the coating links together to form stronger polymer structures when exposed to ultra-violet light, giving a durable ink attracting image.

Plates

After exposure the unexposed coating is washed off with a developer solution and the non-image areas are made water attracting by coating the surface with a gum solution (gum arabic). This gum layer adheres to the grained surface and prevents printing ink from forming on the non-image areas.

Positive-working plates

These are based on photopolymer coatings which become unstable when exposed to ultra-violet light. After exposure the coating is removed by a developer solution leaving the unexposed coating to form the image. The plate is gummed to make it water attracting. Since the plate coating can be destabilized by UV light these plates tend not have the press life which the negative-working plate enjoys. Press runs can however be doubled with some types of plate if they are baked to high temperatures after processing. In this case the polymer coating which forms the image is also a thermoplastic, becoming much harder under the action of heat.

Deletions and corrections

Corrections can be made to the presensitized litho plate after it has been processed. The image can be removed (called a deletion) with a deletion rubber or, more usually, with a deletion fluid which is applied by brush. In both cases it is important that the surface grain of the plate is not damaged in this process and the area must be made water-attracting to prevent the possibility of scumming.

Adding fresh work to the processed plate is possible, but is not a practical proposition due to the time required and the uncertain quality of the added work.

Multi-metal plates

The press life of the conventional presensitized plate is partly determined by the wear the plate will receive from press dampers and inking rollers and by the abrasive fibres on the surface of printing papers and board. Plate manufacturers make claims for their presensitized plates which are always

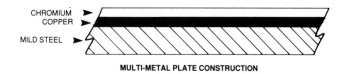

CHROMIUM ➤
COPPER ➤
MILD STEEL ➤

MULTI-METAL PLATE CONSTRUCTION

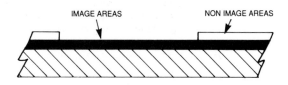

IMAGE AREAS   NON IMAGE AREAS

subject to the factors listed above. Photopolymer plate coatings give longer wear than diazo compound coatings. Thermoplastic-type coatings used for plates which are baked after processing extend the life of the plate something like four times. When plate wear takes place the image which is microscopically higher than its background begins to break down, but so also does the aluminium grained surface. Surface wear varies according to the plate used but with long run negative plates it can begin to appear after 200,000 or so copies have been taken from a plate.

Multi-metal plates owe their development as the answer to plate wear on extended press runs. There are a number of types:

All using presensitized polymer coatings, they consist of a metal base with one or more metals plated to them: copper plated on stainless steel or aluminium, or chromium plated on copper which can be plated to a third metal which becomes the base.

With these plates runs can be in the millions. They also have the advantages of being able to control the dot size and if anything should go wrong on the press acid treatment can restore the plate to its original condition. However, the plates are expensive and as generally print runs are reducing, they tend to be used for the more specialist applications.

Waterless plates

It has always been said that if only one could remove the water from litho printing, the pressmen's lives would be that much easier since they would not need to maintain the ink/water balance, one of the most difficult jobs of litho printing. In fact, a waterless plate was developed a number of years ago but had a number of drawbacks.

However, the technology has been improved and plates are now available, both negative and positive forms, which are claimed to be capable of run lengths in excess of one million impressions without having to bake.

Using the same planographic printing process as litho, a waterless plate uses aluminium for the base and the image inked areas, and silicone rubber for the non-image areas which is cured by exposure. The plate is processed in a similar way to conventional litho plates although it does require a special processor. It can also be necessary to use special printing inks and for the press to be temperature controlled.

On the other hand, due to the elimination of water, excellent print quality can be achieved particularly in terms of strong colours and press waste can be reduced significantly.

Surface-working presensitized plates

These plates are made from mild steel with a surface of grained chromium. A conventional photopolymer/thermoplastic coating on the surface, which is positive-working, is baked hard after processing. The image has a claimed press life of between 800,000 and 1,000,000 and has the advantage over conventional aluminium plates that the non-image areas of the plate do not wear rapidly.

Negative-working multi-steel

The principle of the multi-metal plate is to substitute a metal for photopolymer image coatings and to provide a water-attracting metal for non-image areas of the plate. The latter metal is usually chromium which when grained gives excellent water

carrying properties and a very durable surface. A
number of plate configurations are available:

Base plate metal	Non-image metal	Image metal	Use
Mild steel	Chromium	Copper	Sheet and web presses
Brass	Chromium	Brass	Web presses
Aluminium	Chromium	Copper	Large sheet fed presses

Plates are supplied presensitized and, when exposed
through a negative, the exposed coating softens and
is then removed with developer. This leaves a stencil
on the plate which resists the application of an
etching solution (this operation must be carried out
in a fume extraction facility). The etching solution
removes chromium from all the areas which are to
form an image, thus revealing the underlying copper
which becomes the image (copper and brass have
very good ink attracting qualities). After etching the
stencil is removed and the plate ready for use.

Positive-working multi-metal

The plate configuration is the same as that used for
negative-working plates. In this case however exposure through a positive flat hardens the coating and
when the plate is developed the unexposed areas
(image areas) are free of coating while the rest of the
coating acts as a stencil. This stencil is usually hard-
ened further by applying a hardening solution before
the plate is etched. Etching removes the chromium to
reveal the underlying copper or brass which becomes
the image. After etching the stencil is removed and
the plate is ready for the press.

   With both types of multi-metal plate it is possible
to add patches of chrome to the surface with an
electrolytic kit. This is the method used to remove
unwanted areas which would otherwise print (called
deletion). Adding extra work to the plate after it has
been exposed requires the plate to be recoated and
processed again, but this is not commonly done.

Printing machine configurations

The basic lithographic machine unit consists of a *plate cylinder* onto which the plate is clamped firmly, and a rubber covered cylinder (*blanket cylinder*) which serves to transfer the ink image from the plate cylinder to the paper or stock which is pressed firmly against the blanket cylinder by the *impression cylinder*.

The plate cylinder is supplied with a damping unit which moistens the plate surface before it passes under the inking rollers (*pyramid*). These are fine metering systems which control the amount of water and ink which are applied to the plate during each rotation of the cylinder.

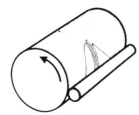

The litho plate is dampened

This is followed by inking

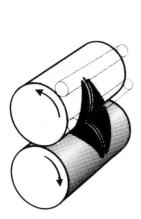

The inked image is transferred (offset) to the blanket cylinder

Paper is impressed against the blanket cylinder by the impression cylinder

Sheetfed machines

These are designed to print on a variety of sheeted stocks: mainly paper and board, but can also be tinplate and plastics.

Single-colour machines

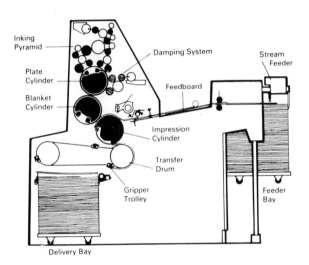

The single machine unit is used to print one colour at a time.

A special mechanism for passing one sheet at a time into the unit (called a *feeder*) is used and another mechanism (called the *delivery*) stacks the sheets neatly after they have been printed.

Single-colour perfector machines

These contain two printing units arranged so that they print the sheet on both sides in one pass through the press. The printing units may be arranged so that the sheet passes between the blanket cylinders which are opposed to each other (*blanket-to-blanket press*).

This type of machine does not have an impression cylinder, the blanket cylinder of one unit acting as the impression cylinder for the other and vice versa. (see below).

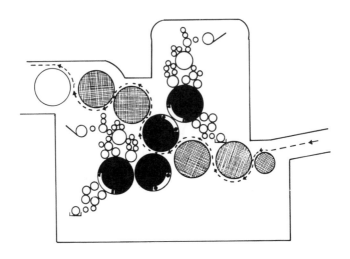

Multi-colour machines

Each multi-colour press has two or more printing units arranged to print onto the sheet as it passes through the press.

In-line machines (tandem) This type of press (above) consists of single units combined together in line to form two, to eight and sometimes ten colour presses. The sheet is conveyed from one unit to another via transfer cylinders.

Modular unit machines This type of machine is

designed as a single modular unit to print two or
more colours and usually has a single impression
cylinder around which two or more printing units are
placed. Two colour modular units may be placed in
line to form a multi-colour tandem press, and a four
colour modular unit (called a *satellite*) may be
placed in-line with another satellite unit to print four
colours on both sides of the sheet in one pass through
the press.

Converter machines

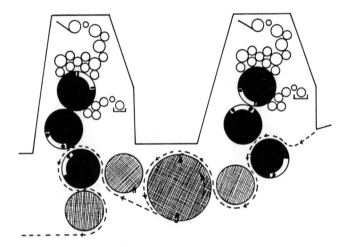

This type of press can consist of two printing units
arranged so that the sheet is printed with two colours
on one side or when *converted* will print one colour
on each side of the sheet in one pass.

If there are four units in the press, this can give
four colours on one side of the sheet, or when
converted two colours on both sides of the sheet in
one pass. Other combinations are possible depending on the position of the perfecting unit which has
special mechanisms incorporated in the transfer
drums allow the sheet path through the press to be re-
routed when the conversion is activated.

Other machine designs

Small-offset machines lend themselves to specialized methods of printing and various press designs have been used to print more than one colour on a simple press. One design has two plate cylinders transferring two separate colours to a single blanket cylinder (no overlapping of colours is possible). Numerous designs allow a second printing unit to add spot colour by letterpress, including numbering and perforating.

Webfed machines

Webfed machines are designed to print on a ribbon or web of paper drawn from a reel. All these machines can print on both sides of the web doing it simultaneously as the web passes between the two blanket cylinders. Alternatively, the blanket-to-sheet press turns the web over between printing units by means of turning bars.

Web presses come in a variety of sizes and are usually designated for specific types of work, e.g. narrow width presses are used for labels and continuous stationery, while magazine presses may print on single-width or double-width webs. A single-width press using a web width which can vary between 875 and 900mm will yield four A4 pages across the web width.

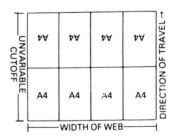

The length of the printed image on the web press is determined by the circumference of the plate cylinder. When the web passes to the folder it is cut into sections by the cutting cylinder and it is this *cutoff* length which identifies the press printing size. Thus a single-width press usually accommodates a web width of about 900mm and a cutoff length of 630mm yielding eight pages to view (16 pages perfected) to each section.

Press configurations vary considerably. A single blanket-to-blanket unit press will yield one colour on both sides of the web. A second unit added to the first will either give two colours on both sides of a single web, or with a separate reel yield two webs printed in one colour both sides. The permutation is obvious. Each added unit can be used for extra colour or an extra web. The following illustrations show some of the possibilities from multiple units.

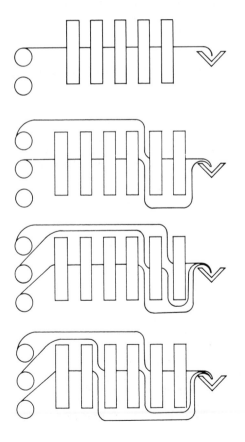

One reel only in use, giving the potential to print full colour plus one 'special' colour – possibly a PMS colour for advertising use – by passing the web through all five units.

The versatility of a six-unit press with three reel stands. Two webs in use, one printed in four colours, the other in two colours: 32pp in all, 16pp in full colour and 16pp in two colours.

Three webs in use producing one 48pp section as 16pp in full colour and 32pp in black.

Three webs in use producing one 48pp section as three 16pp each in black with a different spot colour.

A four unit press with two reel stands. Only one reel is in use and the web passes through only one unit. Equivalent to a single-unit configuration, it will produce 16pp printed in colour, usually black.

The same press loaded with two reels of paper, each passing through one unit. The two webs will be folded together to produce a 32pp magazine section in one colour throughout.

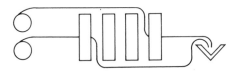

The two webs each pass through two units, each unit printing one colour, thus giving two colours on each side of each web, resulting in a 32pp section printed in two colour throughout.

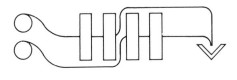

One web passing through all four units giving the potential to print one 16pp section in four colours (ie full process colour) on each page.

A very common configuration: a five unit press with one web in four colours (ie passing through four units) and one in one colour. This will produce a 32pp section with the potential for 16pp to be in full colour and 16pp in black.

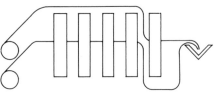

The same press producing one web in three colours and one in two.

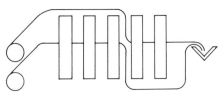

When the web leaves the last printing unit it is drawn into the folder section of the press. This can involve the web passing over a *former* (or kite) which makes the first fold before the web is cut into sections. These are then folded again a number of times until the final page size is achieved. It is then possible for the section to be stitched. It may also be trimmed on three sides (*three-knife-trimmer*) before final delivery by conveyor into the stackers which can stack the sections in predetermined numbers. They can then be packed, addressed and made ready for immediate delivery to the customer.

In the case of bookwork printing, and where superior folding and more accurate cutting of the web are necessary, the web can be slit into ribbons of pages as it advances to the folder. These ribbons are then passed over angled bars (*ribbon folding*) which accurately align the combined ribbons into sections for cutting,

In colour work, it is customary to make up a *flat-plan* of page positions in order to assess the balance of the content and calculate where four colour, two colour or single colour may fall. A typical flat-plan (see next page) will show the contents laid out as 8, 16 or 32 page blocks; and from this the most economical method of positioning the pages for use of colour is obtained.

Specific machine operations carried out in the printing process are summarized here:

Machining operations

Sheetfed machines

Feed and positioning

The feeder. This mechanism is designed to lift single sheets in sequence from the sheet pile and convey them accurately into the printing unit. Sheets are lifted by suction or vacuum suckers and supported through the feeder by air blast and conveyor belts. The single-sheet feeder advances on one sheet at a time to the printing unit, and the stream feeder advance sheets which are slightly overlapping to the printing unit thus speeding up the process.

Most printing machines carry detection devices which cut out the printing if a sheet is missed, is twisted, or if two sheets are picked up.

Lays. These are adjustable stops situated at the front edge and side of the feedboard which determine the position of the sheet as it enters the grippers of the printing unit.

Grippers. A series of metal fingers take hold of the sheet as it lies at the lay stops and pull it through the printing unit and then release it at the delivery pile. Several sets of grippers are used when transferring sheets from one printing unit to another in a multicolour press.

An allowance on the gripper edge of the sheet must be made when assessing the maximum area of printed image. This can vary and needs checking with the printer.

Printing unit

Plate cylinder. This cylinder contains clamps which hold and tension the press plate. The plate can be adjusted both laterally and circumferentially to facilitate registration of the image on the printed sheet. Such registration is made easier if a pin-register system is used.

Damping system. This is designed to produce a fine layer of moisture on the plate surface prior to it passing under the inking rollers. Systems vary: one type uses one or two cloth covered rollers to apply moisture to the plate. These are supplied by other rollers which meter moisture from a fountain roller. Increasingly though alcohol damping is used. These systems also consist of a series of rollers but the fountain solution contains a percentage of Isopropyl Alcohol or its equivalent or an alcohol substitute. Because of the action of alcohol in lowering surface tension, and because it evaporates rapidly, this method of damping uses less plate moisture which means less dimensional change of paper size (due to moisture uptake) than normal damping allows.

A typical flat plan for a magazine.

The correct balance between water on the plate and ink applied to the image is of great importance in lithographic printing.

Inking system. Printing ink is fed into the roller pyramid from an ink reservoir (duct) which meters the ink via a metal blade which is adjustable by screws to control the ink flow. Computer controlled inking systems adjust these screws automatically according to densitometer readings taken from the printed sheet or digitally direct from the printing plate using a scanner. Control is normally from a separate viewing console. As well as establishing correct ink levels for the job in hand, a record of the correct settings can be stored and used to set the press control automatically when the job is re-printed.

Blanket cylinder. The inked plate image is trans-ferred to the blanket which offsets it on to the stock being used. Due to the blanket's resilience, the ink image can be transferred even on to coarse stock with good definition. However, the correct impres-sion pressure is important. Different grades of blan-ket hardness are used to suit various types of stock and press speeds.

Impression cylinder. This is an adjustable cylinder which ensures pressure contact between paper and blanket at the moment of printing. In many cases this cylinder carries a set of grippers which hold the sheet firmly as it passes through the unit.

Transfer

The multi-colour press of modular design can incor-porate a common impression cylinder which holds the sheet of stock firmly while each separate blanket impresses its image on it. Registration problems between one colour and another are therefore mini-mal. The in-line or tandem press however uses a series of transfer drums to support the sheet between one unit and another. The sheet is held by grippers which are on a continuous chain loop from feedboard to delivery, or the sheet may be transferred from one set of grippers to another set on each transfer drum. Both systems have their drawbacks and need to be kept in good condition to maintain sheet register.

Delivery

Final delivery of the printed sheet to the pile is normally by sets of grippers arranged on a short chain loop. The sheet is released over the pile and settles down on a cushion of air supplied by nozzles. At each side of the pile sheet guides called joggers gently nudge the sheet into a final resting position.

Anti-setoff-spray can be applied over the surface of the sheet as it drops to the pile. The minute granules of the spray prevent the sheet making intimate contact with its fellows and thus lower the risk of wet ink transferring between them.

Alternatively, accelerated drying techniques can be used involving either infrared or ultraviolet curing technology, for drying either the inks themselves or an overcoating of thin varnish.

Webfed machines

Feed and positioning

Reel stands. Paper is fed into the web press in a continuous ribbon (or web) of paper pulled off a reel. A web tension device called a *dancer roller* senses variations in web tension and corrects this by applying a brake to the reel.

Originally, when the reel ran out the press had to be stopped and a new reel supplied. With small presses this was of no great disadvantage. However, on larger presses it can be very time consuming particularly when several reel stands are involved. Hence, today, the changing of reels tends to be performed automatically while the press is running. These automatic reel changing devices join a fresh reel of paper to the end of the old web and perform an action of speeding up the new reel to press speed, pasting the leading edge of the new web to the end of the old and slitting the old web from its reel. This entire operation takes a split-second and has earned the device the name of *flying paster*.

Path rollers. Web support between units is given by free rotating rollers. Side lay rollers may be adjusted manually or automatically to keep the web central and to give side lay registration. *Compensa-*

tor rollers are similarly adjustable to control the forwards position of the web and to register multiple webs as they arrive at the folder.

Turner bars form part of the ribbon folder and are used to turn the web at right angles. They are fixed, highly polished and perforated to enable the web to be supported on a layer of air.

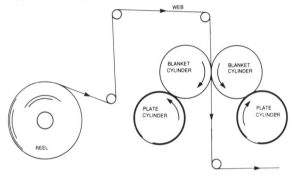

Printing unit

Plate cylinder. Cylinders are designed to take one or more wrap-around plates. In many cases, this brings the leading edge of the plate to within about 30mm of its back edge when it is fitted although with some of the latest presses the gap can be closed altogether. Each plate cylinder is equipped with facilities for moving it laterally and circumferentially for register purposes.

Damping system. The damping system used on the web press functions to the same principle as the sheetfed press. Numerous designs however are used on web presses because high press speeds require a finer application of moisture.

Inking system. Almost the same in design as the sheetfed press, the web press unit however is generally more compact and ink roller pyramids are smaller. Also, due to the larger quantities of inks involved computerized ink pumping systems are not uncommon.

The principle of the web offset press.

Blanket cylinder/impression cylinder. Narrow web presses such as are used for producing continuous stationery and direct mailers may carry separate impression cylinders, but most large web presses function on the blanket-to-blanket principle for impression. Blankets are wrap-around, covering the same area as the plate cylinder.

Delivery

Drying. Inks printed on high speed presses must obtain an initial surface dryness (called *set*) before the web enters the folder. Certain grades of paper (e.g. newsprint) which are highly absorbent are printed with *cold-set* inks which do not require special drying facilities on the web press.

Heat-set inks are required for less absorbent paper and for most multi-colour printing. These inks gain an 'initial set' when subject to high temperatures and the rapid cooling. High temperature drying forces volatile solvents out of the printed ink leaving a gel on the surface which is 'set' by passing the web over a series of refrigerated drums (chill rolls) before it enters the folder. The inks can be dried in a number of ways:

☐ the flame impingement gas oven, in which a naked flame is directed over the web surface as it passes through the drying unit.
☐ the hot air oven contains air jets (air-knives) which direct high velocity hot air onto the web surfaces.
☐ heating of the web surface is obtained by the infra-red drier.
☐ ultra-violet radiation is used in a drying unit to cure special inks.

Folding There are two principal types of web press folding which can also be combined:

☐ former folder
☐ ribbon folder.

With the *former folder* the web is directed over a triangular former (or *kite*) to make the first fold. A knife on a cutting cylinder cuts the folded web to a fixed length – the *cutoff*; and each cut length is folded further as required by a series of cylinders which contain a jaw recess into which the section is forced to complete the fold.

The *ribbon folder* is used for bookwork and high grade multi-colour printing. With this folder the oncoming web is split into ribbons which are aligned into the folder by passing them over turner bars instead of using the former. Web press folders generally work to high standards of tolerance within their capacities, and problems which arise at this stage in the process are more likely to be marking and set-off problems rather than the folding of the paper.

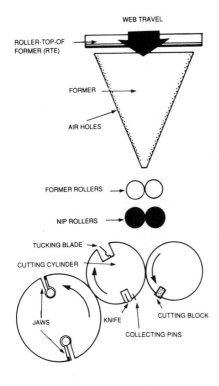

Principle of a former folder.

Choosing the process: sheetfed or webfed offset

☐ Assuming the main considerations to be the best quality for the best price, the factors which will influence the choice of process will be:

☐ economic print run lengths can vary considerably with web runs continuing to decrease and sheet work increase but normally it is not economic to put runs much under 5,000 on a web press.

☐ the higher web press speed will, with its combined folding and finishing section, meet tight deadlines better than the sheetfed press.

☐ Generally, web presses, however, offer only a limited range of standard trim sizes and extents as their final product although this can be overcome if the press has an in-line sheeter. Non-standard sizes and finishing processes are handled better by sheetfed litho.

☐ The production cycle, or length of time on machine, can be a crucial factor in establishing the cost effectiveness of one process over the other. This is particularly true of colour work. Note that most web offset machines deliver perfected, folded sections, and that running speeds are comparatively high. To do the same job sheetfed can involve first printing all the sheets one side only; then backing them all up; then folding them as a separate operation. Unless several machines are used simultaneously, a sheetfed production cycle will normally take longer, and this will be reflected in the price.

☐ Bear in mind that sheetfed and web offset machining prices can never be compared as like for like; the complete picture needs to be seen. Not only does the separate cost of folding need to be added on to the sheetfed price; but the paper consideration can be a determining factor. Paper bought on the reel will be cheaper than the same paper bought in sheets; but web offset paper wastage can be higher than sheet offset wastage, and the total value of the paper that needs to be purchased has to enter the equation.

☐ Note that some specialist web installations can achieve extremely cost-effective production runs as low as a few thousand by standardising paper and formats.

☐ Where price and delivery are even, note that sheet offset printing can sometimes offer more flexibility where either formats or final pagination are not known until a late stage, or where there are possibilities for future small reprints which would need to be printed sheetfed. The question of oddments in magazine or bookwork can be important: oddments can normally be more effectively printed sheetfed, either by using a smaller machine, or by printing on a smaller sheet size.

Special considerations in single-colour litho printing

Textmatter

☐ Note the crucial importance of satisfactory originals.

☐ Assuming satisfactory, consistent originals and properly monitored origination, the printer should have few reasons not to reproduce a satisfactory printed result. Note however that typefaces with delicate hairline serifs (e.g. Bodoni) are more demanding to reproduce and print than more robust, consistently thicker faces (e.g. Plantin), or monoline faces (e.g. Univers). To originate and print such typefaces well is as demanding as originating and printing fine line artwork.

☐ Achieving consistency of colour through the run, and a dense shade of black in normal textwork, are the main challenges.

Half-tones

☐ Proper monitoring of the origination and proofing process is vital. For top quality work it is advisable to see machine proofs on the half-tones, in 'scatter proof' form or in imposed form, and for the proofs to be run with a density strip bar which can be used to assess the ink film thickness and density at press stage.

☐ It is vital that the correct screen ruling has been chosen to match the paper being printed on. Where the screen is too coarse for the paper (100 screen on artpaper, for example), the screen pattern becomes obtrusive. Where too fine a screen has been chosen for the paper (150 screen on cartridge or cheap matt-coated), the ink will spread, giving excessive dot gain, with shadows filling in and highlights turning muddy.

☐ Machine cleanliness, and smooth, firm-surfaced paper are both vital. Imperfections are more visible on single-colour work than even on four-colour work, since only one layer of ink is applied to the sheet, and there are no subsequent layers to hide a defect in one of the other workings.

□ Go for the best possible quality of paper within a budget. A poor paper surface will put a very definite upper limit on the quality of half-tone possible regardless of the quality of origination. Nothing is more dispiriting than to compare a sharp black half-tone proofed on artpaper, with its muddy, flat, dead equivalent if the job is printed on an unsuitable, absorbent paper.

Special considerations in multi-colour litho printing

Textmatter

□ Where textmatter is to print in more than one of the process colours, or is to reverse out of a panel made up of process colour tints or a four-colour half-tone, be sure that the type size is sensibly large, and that the serifs are not too fine. Any delicate typeface reversed out from a number of colours will risk being spoiled. Choose the minimum number of colours possible in reversing to white from a coloured panel.

□ Where textmatter reverses out of a single-colour panel, the same remarks about serifs apply, albeit to a lesser degree. Nevertheless choose robust typestyles where you can.

□ Where type or line is being printed in a special colour outside the process range, use a generally accepted colour code to inform the printer (e.g. a Pantone reference number) and attach a swatch to the artwork as an additional aid.

Half-tones

□ Proper monitoring of the origination and proofing processes is vital. For critical colour work it is essential to see machine proofs of the half-tones proofed with a complete set of colour bars; with a set of progressives made in printing order; with standard inks; on the same stock as will be used for printing.

□ On machine, a comprehensive set of colour controls should be run and constantly monitored to give detailed information on ink hold-out, ink film density, press performance.

☐ Bear in mind the process being used. High speed wet-on-dry printing presents a different set of potential problems from single-colour or two-colour wet-on-dry printing.

☐ Some printers issue technical standards specifying the form in which they require films to be proofed and then supplied, based on their knowledge of their own press performance. Such standards make useful reference checklists for the buyer as well as for the suppliers concerned, and should be obtained where possible.

Such data is commonly given in American trade houses where the trade standard – SWOP (Specification for Web Offset Publications) – has been agreed by consensus of advertising agencies, magazine publishers, graphic arts associations and printers.

The closest standard to SWOP in Europe are the specifications recommended for the publication of colour separations in web offset magazines established by the International Federation of the Periodical Press (FIPP). These are published in the reference section.

Identifying problems

A disappointing printing result must be analysed carefully to pinpoint problem areas and to ensure that the quality of printed work is achieved. Troubleshooting of this nature must follow a consistent pattern:

Check the quality of originals. Poor quality prints may be the fault of poor quality original artwork and illustrations. Faults in originals which may affect the printed result include the following:

In *single-colour work* look out for:

☐ variations in density of typesetting where originals are taken from previously printed matter
☐ variations in density of correction lines with previously set text
☐ shadow lines produced by correction lines in text matter

☐ flat or high contrast tones in photographic originals.

In *multi-colour work* look out for:

☐ over-enlargement of original colour transparencies

☐ colour contrast deficiencies in colour transparencies

☐ colour transparencies contain a wider tonal range than is possible to reproduce.

Check the quality and type of stock supplied for printing. Fine line, half-tone and process colour work printed on a non-coated surface can suffer

---

Specifying standards

Printers' technical standards specifications, if comprehensive, will include the following:

☐ The form in which the film is supplied: positive or negative; composite or non-composite; positioning of register marks and trim marks.

☐ Film emulsion classification: e.g. litho negatives must be reverse-reading.

☐ Screen ruling of half-tones: 120/133/150, etc.

☐ Screen angles required for each colour.

☐ Undercolour removal information: the sum total of overprinted tone values in darkest areas (e.g. 280%).

☐ Dot gain and loss allowance: to compensate for known half-tone reproduction on individual printing machines.

☐ Colour control strips: type used and position on the sheet.

☐ Litho plate exposure control: tolerances.

☐ Colour proofing: method and sequence required (to conform to printing sequence).

☐ Proofing inks: to conform to press inks.

☐ Printed ink densities: established by densitometer control.

☐ Proofing stock: to match stock used for the press run.

---

from ink absorption and consequently appear flat and dull. Cheap matt-coated cartridge with inadequate surface coating can produce the same result. Half-tone screen ruling should be appropriate to the paper chosen.

When printed colour work fails to match machine proofs, check:

☐ printed performance by examination of colour control bars
☐ specifications and colour sequence of colour proofs have been followed
☐ that the same inks and stock used for proofing were used for printing.

Non-impact printing

The technologies which fall into this category are numerous although traditionally the sector has been dominated by electrostatic printing. Developed in the past 40 years, it is commonly used for photocopying. Image definition however is continually improving and certain machines equal the image quality of offset lithography.

The main advantages of electrostatic printing are:

☐ reproduction from an original does not require photographic film or plate

☐ because it is a non-impact printing process the machinery tends to be of lighter weight and is more suitable for office installations than a printing press

☐ the process does not use printing ink and the machines do not require cleaning after each job like normal printing presses

☐ the process has a direct relationship with computer-based systems.

The process

Electrostatic printing technology has changed rapidly in the past 20 years due to the discovery of substances known as photoconductors. The following outline shows the basic principle of electrostatic printing but does not attempt to describe a particular commercial process (all of which are under constant development).

☐ A metal drum which has a photoconductive surface is given an electrostatic charge (the drum is enclosed in the dark)

☐ Pages in digital format are sent to the system's computer or camera-ready artwork is placed in the machine and is illuminated. The reflected image is directed through a lens system on to the charged drum

☐ Where light falls onto the drum surface the electrostatic charge leaks away to leave charged particles only in the image areas of the surface

☐ A resin-based powder (black or colour) is cascaded over the drum surface. The powder has an opposite electrical charge to that which forms the image on the drum. The toner powder settles on the image areas and the rest is removed from the surface

☐ The printing paper is given an electrostatic charge and when brought into proximity with the metal drum, attracts the powder to itself forming an image on the paper

☐ This powder image is heated, causing the resin to melt and fuse with the paper.

Short-run black printing

Short-run printing using the electrostatic process may begin with hard copy originals or with electronic files.

Systems have been developed which are fast challenging the low-end of the litho process and two manufacturers in particular – Kodak and Xerox – are refining systems which are capable of producing books, brochures, etc. to an adequate quality and at speeds which can be faster than litho, taking into account make-ready time. A typical system is the Xerox DocuTech, which can accept input either as hard copy from which a fast scanner transfers the page images into electronic memory or as an electronic file which drives the machine direct.

Software takes care of imposition and positioning and much development is under way to increase both the sophistication and quality of such systems. Printers of short-run books have already installed machines and are producing good quality work at competitive prices and it seems likely that this type of process will supplant a large percentage of conventional short-run litho where the investment in such a system can be justified by high throughput.

Short-run colour printing

Originally, the only economically viable option for short run colour printing was litho. We then saw the introduction of colour copiers which as the technology improved began to be used for the really short runs although when the machines became capable of being driven by rips and accepting digital data the run lengths increased.

However, in 1993, two alternative systems were

Applications

introduced, the E-Print 1000 from Indigo and Xeikon's DCP which Agfa also sells in another form as the Chromapress. Although using somewhat different printing technologies - the Xeikon engine uses dry toner while Indigo has developed a new type of liquid ink - both systems provide good quality full colour work and are best suited to short runs or jobs with changing data.

Both machines accept data in PostScript and a number of other formats either directly or remotely. A digital interface then supplies page information directly to the press, by-passing film, plate, proof and make-ready stages.

The Chromapress uses a continuous web feed (the maximum roll width gives full bleed A3). It prints images simultaneously on both sides of the web as it rises vertically between two sets of four-colour printing units at 600dpi resolution. An integral sheeter cuts to length and the press delivers 1050 four-colour, two-sided A3 sheets per hour.

The E-Print sends images to a single cylinder at a resolution of 800dpi. It is possible to print up to six colours, each laid down by a revolution of the cylinder enabling 4,000 A3 impressions an hour single colour or 1,000 an hour four-colours.

Both systems can conduct basic on-line finishing operations and continue to be developed. In fact, the area of short run colour printing is expected to see a number of innovations, not just with these systems but also ones using electrostatic, ink-jet and other technologies by companies such as Xerox, Canon and Scitex, as well as traditional press manufacturers.

Other processes

Letterpress applications are virtually non-existent, but may still include the following:

☐ printed stationery, letterheads, envelopes (platen printing or possibly small flatbed)
☐ short-run general jobbing print (platen printing, or small flatbed)
☐ short-run magazine and bookwork (small flatbed)
☐ specialist, craft-orientated printing (small flatbed)
☐ medium to long-run paperback books (web rotaries)
☐ certain packaging applications (web rotaries)

The pre-press stages and the eventual surface to be printed from will be dictated by the application sought and the type of printing machine to be used.

A small amount of letterpress printing – where available – will almost certainly be considerably more expensive than litho, and as a purely commercial choice can normally be excluded as a possibility.

For printed stationery in standard formats, letterheads, visiting cards, general short-run jobbing printing, etc., letterpress printing from type can still be a viable commercial option.

Line blocks

Line illustrations in letterpress for making up with type are made by etching a metal plate and mounting this to type-height (0.918") in the forme with the other components.

Half-tone blocks

Tone illustrations in letterpress for making up with type are made by etching a metal plate and mounting this to type-height in the forme with the other components. The plate is normally of copper or of zinc.

Note that before printing from a letterpress forme of metal type and blocks, very substantial make-ready is involved which adds substantially to the cost of the process.

Stereos

In certain newspaper plants where the printing is by webfed rotary letterpress and the typesetting is still hot metal, the printing plates used are stereos. An impression of the type is taken in flexible papier-mâché *flong*; and the curved stereo plate is cast from this, in type metal, and mounted on to the cylinder of the letterpress rotary machine for printing.

Plastic plates/rubber plates

Flexible plastic plates are made by impressing the type forme into a thermosetting plastic to create a mould from which the thermoplastic or rubber duplicates are made under heat and pressure. Like stereos, hot metal composition facilities have declined almost to zero.

Duplicates from CRC/film

Photopolymer plates made from CRC or film took over from the previous two processes for webfed rotary letterpress applications, mainly for long-run book and newspaper production.

Several patent systems were developed of which the best known are APR, Letterflex and Nyloprint. All are materials which when contacted to right-reading film produce a raised, relief image on a flexible, photopolymer base, for mounting on foils to print rotary web.

The development of such plates meant that letterpress was able to continue as a cost-effective process for printing in some of its traditional areas even though hot-metal typesetting had been completely displaced by filmsetting.

Letterpress printing machines

Conventional letterpress machines are designed on one of three principles:

Platen principle

The forme is held in a vertical type-bed. Impression is carried out by the platen, a heavy metal plate which swings forward and upward in an arc, carrying the paper, and impressing it into the surface of the forme as it reaches a position where it is vertical and parallel with the forme.

Flatbed (cylinder) principle

The type-bed is flat and horizontal. Positioned over it is the cylindrical impression cylinder on which the paper to be printed is held. Impression is carried out as the bed moves in a horizontal direction under the revolving cylinder on the impression stroke; the impression cylinder lifts to allow the bed to return to its first position; and the cycle is repeated.

Rotary principle

The printing surface consists of either curved stereos or flexible plastic, rubber or photopolymer plates, which are fixed around the circumference of the plate cylinder. An impression cylinder rotates against the plate cylinder and impression is carried out as the paper (sheets or reels) is fed between them. One letterpress machine, designed for paperback and cased book production, departs from conventional patterns: the Cameron, a 'complete book' machine. Printing is from photopolymer plates imposed on long continuous belts, several pages in width. The process is webfed; collation is by web being slit into a number of superimposed ribbons which are chopped into single leaves; and the other book-binding processes follow on in-line.

Gravure

Gravure is an *intaglio* printing process, in which the image to be printed is etched into the surface of a copper cylinder. Printing is achieved by flooding the surface of the cylinder with ink which fills the intaglio image areas, wiping away ink in the non-image areas of the cylinder, and then impressing the web of paper against the surface of the cylinder. Under impression, the ink in the intaglio areas is transferred to the paper.

In the development of the process three types of cylinder preparation have been used:

Conventional cell gravure

This method formed cells in crossline formation of equal size but varying depth. The thickness of ink printed corresponded with the depth of the cells. This process was the original method of cylinder preparation but is now obsolete.

Invert half-tone

This method is now the most widely used method for magazine and catalogue printing. The steps in the process are as follows:

☐ a fully prepared make-up in either film or print form is mounted on the scanning unit drum or flatbed

☐ the entire make-up is scanned, the photo-electric monitor picking up light reflected from the surface or light passing through the film

☐ this is converted into signals which are processed by a computer to control an engraving stylus which cuts into the copper surface of the cylinder

☐ the cells so produced are of varying depth and size

☐ after completion and final inspection, the cylinder may be chromium plated to give it longer life.

Variable area direct transfer

The cylinder is prepared in a similar way to invert half-tone cylinders, but each cell has a constant depth (usually deeper than invert half-tone). This method is used mainly for textile printing and packaging.

The process

Origination and cylinder preparation costs are relatively high in gravure which means that the process is economically suitable for runs of no less than 250,000 copies. Although sheet-fed gravure presses are manufactured, the majority are high speed webfed machines. The printing process is mechanically simple. The printing cylinder is partially immersed in an ink bath, and as it revolves ink in the non-image areas is removed by a flexible steel blade called a doctor blade. The web of paper passes between the copper cylinder and a rubber-covered impression roller to receive the print and then passes through a drier unit before entering the folder. The web controls and handling are similar to those used for web offset.

Applications

The main applications for gravure are for these products:

☐ long run magazine, brochure and catalogue printing in full colour
☐ long run packaging, textile printing, wallpaper printing, etc.
☐ long run security printing of stamps, cheques, banknotes, share certificates, etc.

Flexography

Flexography could be described as a combination of relief letter press and gravure in that it uses flexible rubber or photopolymer plates on web fed rotary presses and a fluid ink which dries quickly by solvent evaporation in a drier unit. Flexo presses are usually large installations with several printing units, dedicated to one specialized form of work. Print runs tend to be on the long side but are reducing.

The process

Production of the rubber or photopolymer plates for this process are identical with letterpress platemaking. Since the plates are flexible they are easily attached with adhesive tape to the printing cylinder since impression pressures tend not to be as critical as with the metal letterpress plate. This allows rapid press make-ready. Flexo plates are hard wearing and in some applications half-tone and multi-colour work are used. The flexible plate tends to distort slightly under pressure and image squash is characteristic. Designs for flexo printing must take these features into consideration.

Applications

Flexography has found wide application in printing for food packaging with plastics and non-absorbent stocks. It also has wide application in printing on low cost wood pulp papers such as for sacks and corrugated board. Other applications include cheap magazines and paperback books, and due to technical developments more recently for newspaper production.

Screen printing

Screen printing is a development of the stencilling process. It is often incorrectly referred to as 'silk screen' printing. The name derives from its handcraft origins when the stencil-supporting screens were made from silk. Silk screens do still have a limited use in the production of fine art prints, where the creative techniques of serigraphy (silk drawing) are often employed. Here the name silk screen or serigraphy clearly signifies certain qualitative associations.

In modern commercial and industrial screen printing screens are made from synthetic or metal gauzes which have the requisite properties of high stability and durability necessary for machine production. Although semi and fully automatic machinery is widely used the process is ideally suited for short and medium run work, also making it suitable for hand-bench operation.

Depending on the particular application the table following shows the production methods which may be employed, but bear in mind that this data is related to sheetfed machinery; web machine configurations, used in the production of labels, touch-panel switches, and printed textiles are capable of a wider range of production speeds.

Method	i.p.h.	run length
Manual hand-bench	150–200	1–1000
Semi-automatic	600–1000	1000–10000
3/4 automatic	1200–1500	5000–10000
Fully-automatic (flat bed)	1500–2000	5000–15000
Fully-automatic (cylinder)	2500–5000	7000+

The process

The relatively simple method of ink transfer on which the process is based involves forcing the ink through the image-forming apertures of the stencil/screen on to the stock beneath. This is usually effected with the use of a rubber, plastic or spring steel blade (squeegee).

The non-impact principle of ink transfer gives the process the capability to:

☐ print on to almost any substrate
☐ print on to curved and uneven surfaces
☐ produce very thick, opaque ink film deposits (10-15 microns)
☐ produce brilliantly saturated colours with lightfastness ratings of 6-8 on the blue wool scale
☐ produce ink films with high chemical and abrasion resistance.

The screen has two functions:

☐ to provide a supportive structure for the stencil
☐ to meter the ink film deposit.

Screens are made by tensioning a fine gauze material over a wooden or metal frame. Screens are usually tensioned to precise gauze specifications, using mechanical or pneumatic tensioning devices. This ensures evenness of tension and controlled dimensional stability.

A wide variety of machines is in use, ranging from flat-bed presses to various types of cylinder and rotary machine.

Some are highly automated while others are virtually entirely manual.

Applications

Among the many diverse applications of screen printing the following catagories may be usefully identified:

- □ *Graphics*
  Display and point of sale advertising
- □ *Posters*
  Vehicle markings
  Self adhesive labels, transfers and stickers
  Signs, flags and banners
- □ *Surface Decoration*
  Imprinted sports and leisure wear
  Fashion and furnishing fabrics
  Floor and wall coverings
  Ceramic tiles and ceramic ware
  Glass decoration
- □ *Markings*
  Hats, caps and bags
  Nameplates
  Business gifts and novelty items
  Folders and binders
- □ *Industrial Applications*
  Printed circuits
  Membrane switches
  Instrumentation
  Bottles and containers
  3-D objects

Die stamping

Die-stamping is the traditional method of producing a relief image on paper or board. Its modern counterpart is thermography, but unlike that process die-stamping is considered to give a superior finish, embossing both sides of the sheet. It also has the advantage of being used for multi-colour images in close register. When used without printing ink (or blind) a simple embossed logo can give a unique effect to notepaper, etc.

The process

A steel die is made photographically, or by etching, engraving or manually. Methods of die-production can be similar to letterpress blockmaking with the image intaglio and not in relief (a female die). Separate dies are made for each separate colour required. In the die-stamping press the die is positioned face uppermost and the paper for printing is placed between the die and its counterpart – the male die made from card. Impression has the effect of forcing the paper into the female die, the force impression being adjusted until the male produces the finest detail from the female die. Inking of the die takes place before each impression. Power presses are fitted with automatic feed and inking, and printed sheets may be dried by an infra-red unit.

Applications

The normal application of die-stamping is to produce prestige letterheads, notepapers, envelopes, invitation cards, wedding stationery, programmes, etc. Multi-colour work using metallic foils can be done by this process. Unlike thermography, die-stamping does not produce problems in laser printers. The best paper and board for die-stamping contain rag fibres, but it can produce a suitable finish on most paper stocks.

Thermography

Thermography is the modern counterpart to die-stamping. It produces a raised image, usually glossy, with no embossed image on the reverse of the sheet.

The process

The thermographic print is produced by dusting a freshly printed image (in the required colour) with a transparent thermosetting powder. The powder sticks to the wet ink and the rest is removed (usually by vacuum.) The sheet is then passed under a heater which softens the powder and causes it to swell slightly to produce a relief image. High-gloss, semi-gloss and matt finishes are available. The amount of raise given to the image can be adjusted by selecting different size granules.

Hand dusting is naturally slow and print runs are limited. Automatic systems are faster when the thermographic unit is in-line with the printing press.

Multi-colour thermography is possible. Soft absorbent papers are not recommended. Hard-sized papers and rag-based papers hold their colour better under heat than papers containing wood pulp. This is especially true where large solids (which require more heat) are included in the image. Cast-coated papers may distort under heat, but relative success may be obtained with one-sided cast-coated board. Ivory and matt boards are recommended.

Applications

Thermography is used for a wide variety of stationery applications where a 'quality' feel can be produced by a raised image, but it should be noted that due to heat involvement, a special powder is required when using thermographed business stationery in laser printers.

7 Paper

Choosing a suitable paper

Type of paper required for any particular job is, of course, governed by the product itself, but there are also printing requirements to take into consideration.

Printing process requirements

☐ *Sheetfed offset litho* Good surface strength, good dimensional stability.

☐ *Web offset litho* Must have a lower moisture content than for sheetfed litho. Similar to the above.

☐ *Sheetfed letterpress* Printing smoothness, absorbency, opacity and compressibility.

☐ *Rotary letterpress* Similar to above.

☐ *Gravure* Printing smoothness is the most important property in this process, should not contain abrasive material.

☐ *Silk screen* Papers should not be too absorbent.

These are the main varieties of paper available, defined by furnish:

Paper varieties

Mechanical

Usually printed letterpress, web offset litho, gravure or flexo, mechanical papers are produced from the cheapest of all the pulps (wood fibres ground mechanically – rather than reduced by chemicals – in the making process). They include newsprint, cheap printings, wallpapers, tissues, cardboards.

Mechanical papers have high bulk, good formation, good dimensional stability and very good opacity but tend to be weak and to lose their strength and colour on ageing. Contain shive. Can be bleached to approximately 70% brightness. Part mechanical can also be coated for use in magazines and as cheap printing paper. Substances available are normally right through the range.

Part mechanical

Used for cheaper printings and writings and are somewhat stronger than papers made from 100% mechanical pulps. Part-mechanical papers contain a significant percentage of sulphate (chemically reduced) pulp to give them added strength, and they may be printed litho as well as letterpress and gravure. The proportion of chemically-made ('woodfree') to mechanical pulp in a part-mechanical paper varies with the grade required. Part-mechanical papers can also be coated to improve ink hold out and so produce an improved print finish.

Woodfree

These are papers which contain only chemically produced pulp or near wood free which contain less than 10% mechanically produced pulp. The properties of the papers vary according to the type of pulp used, the amount of stock preparation, the type and quantity of additives used and the finish that the paper might receive. Papers made with any of these furnishes may have a number of finishes which include:

Machine finished (MF)

A paper which has been mechanically treated on the paper-making machine to improve the smoothness and uniformity on both sides.

Matt coated

The base paper is coated with a coating slick which can be china clay, satin white, etc. This gives improved surface smoothness and ink hold out to the paper.

Gloss coated

Paper which has received this type of finish is also known as art paper. The coating is applied, then the web is passed between a series of rolls, alternately highly polished steel and fibre packed. This gives the paper a very smooth surface with a high gloss finish.

Machine glazed (MG)

A paper which has been dried against a highly polished drying cylinder known as a MG cylinder. This gives one side of the paper a smooth glossy appearance while the other remains relatively rough.

Chromo paper

A paper which is coated and then super calendered (polished) on one side only.

Cast coated paper

A paper which is coated in the conventional way but with the coating dried by passing the wet coated web around a highly polished drying cylinder. This form of coating gives an improved gloss finish to the surface of the web.

Other furnishes

Esparto

Has high bulk and opacity, good smoothness and dimensional stability, good formation and good compressibility. Mainly used for high quality printings and for coating base. Softwood pulps or rag fibres are often included in the furnish to improve strength.

Manilla

Very strong fibres producing very strong paper. Mainly used for envelopes, wrappings, etc.

Cotton (rags)

Usually used to impart softness, permanence, durability, dimensional stability, bulk and opacity. It is used in high quality writings, ledgers and currency papers.

Specialist papers

Kraft

Produced from bleached or unbleached sulphates, it is the strongest of all pulps. Used mainly for wrappings but kraft pulp can be added to other furnishes to increase strength.

Hand-made paper

Furnish is usually cotton, in the form of rags or cotton linters. Hand-made paper has good dimensional stability, random fibre orientation and good permanence and durability. It is extremely expensive to make, so is mostly used by artists for water colour painting or for other specialist jobs.

NCR paper (Carbonless)

'No Carbon Required' paper produces copies by pressure on the top sheet and is made with special coatings on the appropriate sides of the sheets in the set. Pressure breaks the capsule coating pigments and the image is transferred to each sheet where two pigment coatings are in contact. Used for delivery notes, invoices, order forms, etc.

Heat seal paper

Uses a heat-activated adhesive coating. Activation can either be instantaneous or delayed where direct heat may damage the surface or product. Used for labels, etc.

Self-adhesive paper

Applied to a silicon coated backing sheet from which the still sticky paper can be peeled off when ready for contact application.

Gummed paper

Coated with an adhesive which is activated by water. There are two types: 'conventional paper' and 'dry particle gummed', where the particles of adhesive are suspended in an emulsion.

7

Boards

Unlined chipboard

Relatively cheap, made entirely from waste paper. Grey-coloured and used where appearance is not important. Contains a large amount of shive. Usually used for tube winding, ridged boxes, etc.

Lined chipboard

Types include white lined chipboard; Kraft lined chipboard; cream lined chipboard; brown lined chipboard.

Straw board

Produced from unbleached straw pulp by light chemical treatment. Digestion is usually with slaked lime (calcium hydroxide). Its applications include envelope-backing postal stiffener material, boards for hardback books, etc.

Pulp board

Made completely from chemical woodpulp, sometimes on an inverform type machine. This grade might be used for food packaging. Wood free coated board might be used for paperback covers, brochures, greeting cards, etc. Thicknesses generally range from 190–410 µm. Pulpboard can also be cast coated for use with high quality products such as cosmetics and toiletries.

Artboard

Made in the same way as art paper except that board weights usually start above 200–225g/m^2.

Paper ordering

A formal order form is preferable if ordering paper regularly. Publishers ordering paper for delivery to their printers should always confirm the printer's requirements. The following checklists may be helpful.

Specifying sheets

☐ Title of job (book, magazine, etc.).
☐ Paper name.
☐ Quantity of sheets.
☐ Substance.
☐ Caliper.
☐ Long/short grain.
☐ Printing process.
☐ Number of colours to be printed.
☐ Packing: ream wrapped or bulk packed on pallets.
☐ Delivery: see web offset.
☐ Marking: see web offset.

Specifying paper for web offset

☐ Maximum diameter of reels.
☐ Maximum reel width.
☐ Maximum reel weight.
☐ Substance.
☐ Caliper.
☐ Meterage on the reel.
☐ Splices: normally no more than two per reel, taped both sides and giving parallel edges after the join.
☐ Winding: normally wire side out, tight and even with no baggy centres or edges.
☐ Wrapping: normally wrapped in waterproof paper with ends protected by cardboard, suitable for vertical stacking if necessary.
☐ Marking: you will normally want paper name, substance, weight, reel number, direction of winding, name of publication or publisher, if appropriate.
☐ Delivery: delivery notes should carry all information marked on the reel. Time and date of delivery should be arranged with printer.
☐ Imperfections: there should be no cuts, nicks or edge damage and the sheet should be free from slitter dust.

Paper problems

Hickies Can occur with any of the main printing processes. They are random spots on the printed surface, each consisting of a dark spot surrounded by a white halo, and they are caused by solid particles of ink skin, paper debris, damper roller lint or debris from the ink rollers which attach themselves to the printing surface.

The remedies might include: change ink; change damper covers; fit hickey removing device. Run paper through blind; change paper.

Lint or debris piling Mainly occurs with letterpress and litho, and usually occurs when running uncoated grades. Loose fibres on the paper surface are picked up by the blanket, which in turn breaks up the print reproduction on the following sheets.

Remedies: decrease ink tack; reduce press speed; use vacuum brush on press feed board or increase water feed to plate.

Surface picking Can occur on letterpress and lithoprinting process. The fibre or the coating of the paper is lifted from the surface. This can be due to too high an ink tack or insufficient binder in the paper stock.

Remedies: reduce ink tack; reduce press speed; increase impression cylinder pressure; use a harder blanket; increase water supply to the dampers; change paper stock.

Dry Ink Rub/Chalking Occurs mainly with letterpress and litho printing processes and with coated papers. The dried print can be rubbed and so causes the print to smudge. This problem occurs because the ink vehicle drains into the paper, leaving the pigment with insufficient binder; or because the paper is particularly abrasive. Most matt coated papers in particular display abrasive qualities.

Remedies: change ink or reduce ink tack; reduce water supply to damper; reduce acidity of fountain solution; over-varnish.

Mottle Can occur on any printing process. The print, especially in solid areas, appears to be blotchy.

Printing defects associated with paper

This can be due to uneven absorption characteristics of the paper stock, or poorly formulated ink.

Remedies: increase ink tack; reduce supply of ink; increase blanket to impression pressure; change the ink or change the paper.

Set-off Can occur on most printing processes. Traces of the ink on the printed side of a sheeet are transferred to the back of the following sheet in the delivery pile.

Possible remedies include: reduce delivery stack height; use quick set inks; use a paper with higher absorbency characteristics; use an anti-setoff spray or use a delivery pile spacer.

Ink-rub Is associated particularly with illustrated work printed on matt art paper. The ink on the sheet stays wet too long, causing set-off/smudging either in the delivery pile or in the later stages of the finishing/binding process. Some papers are worse than others in this respect.

Remedies include: add liquid driers to the ink; use anti set-off spray; reduce delivery pile height; reduce quantity of ink or change type of ink; change paper to as near a neutral pH paper as possible.

Show-through The printed image can be seen through from the opposite side of the sheet, due to the opacity of the paper being too low for the type of job being printed.

Strike-through The effect is similar to show-through except that it is caused by ink penetrating through the sheet.

Remedies: use a less absorbent paper; reduce the printing pressure; adjust the ink supply; use quick set ink.

Ghosting Can occur on most printing processes. The printed image on one side of the paper appears as a ghost on the printed image of the other side. This is due to chemical ingredients in the first print affecting the wetability characteristics of the reverse side of the paper.

Blade scratches Only occur on blade coated papers

and are caused by dirt or coating mix getting caught under the doctor blade on the coating machine, and causing a fine channel to be formed.

Remedy: change the paper stock.

Distortion This can be in the form of wavy or tight edges in a stack or reel of paper:

☐ *wavy edges* caused by the stack having a lower moisture level than the surrounding atmosphere. Therefore the paper takes in moisture from the atmosphere and in so doing causes the edges of the sheets to go wavy.

☐ *tight edges* caused by the stack having a higher moisture level than the surrounding atmosphere. Therefore the paper gives out some of its moisture to the atmosphere and in so doing causes the edges of the sheets to become tight and the centre of the sheets to become baggy.

Creasing An uneven moisture content in the sheet causes creases at the edges and back of the printed area. If the edges are wavy, creases tend to occur on leave edge corners; if tight, creases tend to occur in the centre of the sheet.

The remedy is to leave packed paper to adjust to room temperature before opening. Open at the last minute and protect during passes.

Tail end hook Is caused by the paper adhering to the blanket too tightly when pulled off by the delivery grippers.

Remedy: use of a heavier paper or adjustments to ink tack, blanket or dampers.

Web breakage Can be caused by excessive tension on one or both edges due to loss of moisture and shrinkage; wrinkles, slime spots or any type of rupture; poor splicing.

Reel defects

Burst reel Caused by the reel having been wound with too much tension.

Remedy: remove outer laps of the reel or if the burst is too deep, reject the reel.

Telescoped reel Due to the reel being wound with insufficient tension.

The only remedy is to have the reel rewound.

Reel out of round Caused by the reel being stored on its side. It can cause misregister when printing, due to the variation in tension that will occur.

The only remedy is to make sure reels are stored correctly on end.

Web wrinkles Due to the web having slack edges through moisture pick-up while still in the reel.

Chain marks Caused by uneven caliper from one edge to the other. The reel will be travelling at slightly different speeds from one edge to the other causing the paper to twist slightly and so cause a distortion in the form of chain marks.

Measurement and calculation

Useful metric units and symbols

Area	square metre	m²
Dimensions	millimetre	mm
	centimetre	cm (1cm=10mm)
	metre	m (1m=100cm=1000mm)
Grammage	grams per square metre	g/m² or gsm
Mass	gram	g
	kilogram	kg(1kg=1000g)
	tonne	t(1t=1000kg=1000000g)
Thickness	micrometre, micron	µm
	millimetre	mm(1mm=1000µm)
Bursting strength	kilopascal	kPa
Internal tearing strength	millinewton	mN
Temperature	degrees Celsius	˚C
Relative humidity	percentage	%
Sheet count	standard ream	500 sheets
Machine direction	indicated by symbol (m)	
	e.g. 640 x 900 (m)	long grain sheet
	640 (m) x 900	short grain sheet
	900 x 640	short grain sheet

Paper sizes

Sheets are usually specified by either an internationally agreed range of the International Standards Organization (A, B, C series); or a range of metric variations on the old Imperial sizes (mostly for bookwork).

The international ISO range

Covered by British Standard BS4000 1983:

☐ it is based upon three series of interrelating sizes designated A, B and C

☐ the sides of the sheet are always in the ratio 1:√2

☐ subdivision from one size to the next one down is denoted by a higher numeral and is made by halving the length of the longest side (e.g. A2 is half of A1).

Trimmed size is defined as: the final dimensions of a sheet of paper.

Untrimmed size is defined as: the dimensions of a sheet of paper, untrimmed and not specially squared, sufficiently large to allow a trimmed size to be obtained from it as required.

A series

A series are trimmed sizes designed for standard printing and stationery needs.

A0 = 1 sq m; A1 = .5 sq m and so on.

Paper sizes are given in the General Reference Section (Section Nine).

Weight and volume (the metric system)

Substance

Paper weight or *substance* is defined as the weight in grams of one square metre of one sheet of paper (i.e. an A0 size sheet) and reported as grams per square metre (abbreviated to g/m^2).

Volume

Paper *volume basis* (a measure of *caliper* or thickness) is the measure of thickness in millimetres of 100 sheets of the paper in 100g/m^2. As a unit of measurement it is referred to as *volume*; abbreviated to *vol.* For example, for a vol 16 paper: 100 sheets of 100g/m^2 of the paper will have been measured as 16mm thick.

Alternatively, the caliper of a single sheet is measured in *micrometres* (μm). As a form of measurement for paper it is only commonly used on the continent.

However, board is sold by thickness rather than weight and this is normally measured as the thickness of a single board in micrometres, although it can sometimes be measured in millimetres.

Standard stock thicknesses are: 200, 230, 250, 280, 300, 400 and 500μm.

Sheets

Calculations

Calculating the number of sheets required for a job

Sheets required =

$$\frac{\text{pages} \ \text{x} \ \text{print run}}{\text{pages per perfected sheet}}$$

Plus allowance for overs

Calculating the weight of paper in the job

Stage 1

$$\frac{\text{mm} \ \text{x} \ \text{mm} \ \text{x} \ \text{g/m}^2}{10^6}$$

$$= \text{kgs/100 sheets}$$

Stage 2

$$\frac{\text{kgs/1000} \ \text{x} \ \text{sheets required}}{10^6}$$

$$= \text{weight of paper in the job (tonnes)}$$

Calculating the weight of a magazine or book

$$\frac{\text{mm} \ \text{x} \ \text{mm} \ \text{x} \ \text{g/m}^2 \ \text{x} \ \frac{1}{2} \ \text{pages}}{10^6}$$

$$= \text{weight (grams)}$$

Add 20 grams for a paperback cover. Add 100 grams for a hardback case.

Number of sheets in a tonne

$$\frac{10^6}{kgs/1000}$$

= number of sheets in one tonne

Reel calculations

Calculating the meterage required for a job

1. Meterage for one section = machine cut-off(m) x printrun plus allowance for overs
2. Meterage for whole job = number of sections in the job x meterage per section

Calculating the weight of this meterage

$$\frac{m \ x \ m \ x \ g/m^2}{10^6}$$

USA measurement and calculation

Most of the world uses the metric system of grams and metres outlined above. The main exception to this is the United States of America whose system still retains much in common with Britain's old Imperial system.

Thus standard units of measurement for weight are: pounds, hundredweights (100lbs) and tons (2000lbs). Paper size is measured in inches and quantity in reams (500 sheets unless otherwise specified).

Weight and size information

Substance is identified by *basis weight.*

Basis weight = weight (lbs) of a ream of paper cut to its *basic size.*

A paper's basic size depends on its grade. The basic sizes for the common paper grades are:

Paper	Basic size (inches)	Equivalent in mm
Cover boards	20 x 26	508 x 660
Newsprint	24 x 36	610 x 914
Book papers	25 x 38	635 x 965

A book paper of basis weight 60lb is written as 25 x 38–60 (500).

Grammage and basis weight conversion

For the most common 25" x 38" basic size papers the factors to retain are:

lbs to g/m^2 : multiply by 1.4800
g/m^2 to lbs : multiply by 0.6757

Substance number

The term substance number is sometimes used as an alternative to basis weight, particularly for bond or writing papers. For example, a bond paper with basis weight 20lb can also be called 'substance 20'.

M weight

Basis weight is often converted into the weight of 1000 (M) sheets (instead of a ream or 500 sheets). So a book paper with a basis weight of 60lb has an M weight of 120lbs.

For a book paper of basis weight 60lb this would be written as:

$$25 \times 38—120(M)$$

instead of

$$25 \times 38—60(500)$$

Prices

Usually expressed as dollars per 100lbs (divide by 100 to give price per lb).

8 Finishing

General operations

These are the more common operations associated with general print-finishing:

folding	inserting
scoring	loose-leaf insertion
bundling	tipping-in
perforating	padding
gathering	guarding
cutting/trimming	counting
collating	punching
index cutting	packing
insetting	drilling
banding	wrapping

Folding

The folding scheme needed to achieve the final printed and finished result required must be decided and advised to the printer in detail, in advance so that an agreed imposition is used. Imposition schemes for leaflets, folders, promotional material, maps and other more unconventional requirements are available from some folding machines but not on others, so pre-planning is vital.

Three basic designs of sheet folder are in use:

☐ the knife folder
☐ the buckle folder
☐ the combination folder.

Among the more common makes of folder in general use are MBO, Stahl and Brehmer.

Knife folders

Were more commonly used in bookwork than for general applications being supremely accurate but are slow and are now mainly replaced by combination machines. The sheet is folded by a blunt-edged or perforated knife which descends and presses the sheet between two inward-rotating wheels which form the paper into a nip. Knife folding is particularly appropriate for successive right-angle folds, or where the stock is particularly thick or thin, and the facility to perforate simultaneously and expel the air prevents creasing.

Buckle folders

Are commonly used for all-purpose finishing as well as for some magazine and bookwork and are capable of very fast running speeds. Folding is carried out by a series of 'plates' with stops which allow a sheet to enter a predetermined distance before being stopped and buckled back at the folding line by two inward-revolving rollers, which nip the sheet and carry it forward, to the next plate.

Combination folders

Combine both knife and buckle techniques and are common all-purpose machines.

Controlling quality

When controlling quality in folding, note the following points:

☐ where the folding appears to be out of square, check the print register as well as the margins. Clearly, where the print is out of register or out of alignment page with page, or does not back up accurately, folding will inevitably show up the defect

☐ buckle folders are not always as accurate as knife folders in folding very light or very heavy papers

☐ creasing is a common symptom of trouble

☐ faults often occur when a buckle folder is run too fast. The sheet then tends to bounce off the stop and fold back in the wrong place: or alternatively it may buckle and crease as it goes through the nip rollers

☐ bear in mind the economies possible, in suitable cases, from web offset printing and 'in-line' folding, which thereby completely eliminate a separate cost for the folding process.

Single-sheet jobs will often go straight from folding to guillotining, after which the job is completed. Multi-sheet jobs will need to go to bundling/gathering and other operations after each section is folded.

Bundling

Bundling is the compression of folded sections in a special bundling machine in order to squash them flat by expelling the air before further processing.

It is an operation which is sometimes omitted; but particularly in cases where sections are to undergo several later print-finishing operations, it can forestall a whole range of potential problems.

Gathering

Where a job consists of several sections of components, the elements must be brought together into the correct sequence to make up the job. Note that this can often be done best by hand in the case of small quantities although gathering machines are normally used for larger quantities. Gathering machines work on the conveyor-belt principle. Piles of sections of the same sort are placed in stations (*hoppers*) along the belt in section sequence, and one of each section is fed on the belt sequentially to make up one copy of the complete job.

Where a job is to be gathered in sections for sewn binding or for perfect binding, the sections are gathered sequentially one on to the side of the next on a flat belt; where the job is to go for saddle stitching, the sections are gathered one over the next, on a saddle with the shape of an inverted V, for final stitching and trimming. Gathering machines normally incorporate trip mechanisms which detect a misfeed and cut out the machine, so faults in gathering more often occur where the work is done by hand. In magazine and bookbinding operations, a 'gatherer-stitcher' is often used, which combines saddle-stitching and trimming in-line with the gatherer conveyor-belt, thus achieving finished articles in one pass.

Collating

The term is often used loosely to mean 'gathering' particularly when individual sheets rather than sections are being combined in a specific sequence using a sheetfeed collator: However, in the strict sense, collating means the checking of gathered sections to ensure that they are in the right order. Collation is normally carried out by checking *black-step* (or *back step*) collation marks – printed marks on the back of each section placed in a predetermined position so that when sections are gathered the black steps fall in a stepped progression down the backs in a quick and easy visible check. In bookwork black-step collation marks will often include the signature identifier – A,B, C, etc. – as an additional check.

Insetting

Insetting is the placing and affixing of one section within another. In gathering saddle-stitched work of uneven extent, the preference is to place larger sections inside small ones: e.g. for a 52pp brochure or magazine, to place a 32pp inside a 16pp inside an odd 4pp. Special insets may be reply-paid cards, special advertising features, etc., as well as regular text sections.

Inserting

Inserting is the placing of a loose piece of paper, or piece of printed material, inside a section/magazine but without affixing it. Such loose inserts can be either positioned at random or, for extra cost, placed in a specific position determined by the customer. Inserting is done either by hand or by machine.

Tipping-in

Tipping-in refers to the affixing of a single leaf inside a section by pasting down a strip along the back edge. Traditionally, it has been done by hand, and is particularly laborious (and consequently expensive) if the position of the tip-in dictates that the 'bolt' in the section must be slit (i.e. the fold between the relevant pages of the section must be slit with a knife at the head or foot) before the tip-in can be affixed. However, machines are now available which can handle the operation automatically.

Tipping-on refers to the affixing of a single leaf to the outside of a section or printed article by the same strip paste method. Thus endpapers are tipped on to the first and last sections of a book; an illustration is tipped on to a calendar. It is often possible to mechanize tipping-on, and sometimes tipping-in so the imposition proposed, in detail, must always be taken into account when planning any job involving tips.

Guarding

A guard is a strip of stout liner made either to be attached to the back of a single leaf and then wrapped round the outside of a section in order to secure the single leaf into a book; or used as a reinforcement to be attached to the folded back of a section in order to strengthen it.

In the case of a single leaf, guarding is an expensive but secure alternative to tipping-in.

In the case of section reinforcement, it is often advisable to guard the first and last section of particularly heavy reference books or dictionaries where there is considerable stress on these two sections when the book is continuously handled.

Punching

Punches are used to create the holes needed in loose-leaf or similar work when relatively small quantities of sheets or leaves are being processed. Larger quantities normally need drilling.

Drilling

Hollow drills are needed to drill through larger quantities of sheets or leaves when dealing with loose-leaf or similar work.

Scoring

Heavy stock and board often needs scoring before it can be folded. A common example is the scoring of covers in paperback or magazine work as they are fed into the wrapper or covering machine to fold around the sections. Scoring that is too heavy can lead to cracking along the score line when the board is folded; scoring that is too light may be insufficient to prevent 'feathering' along the crease when the board is folded. Note too that the best results are obtained when the scores are parallel to the grain direction of the board.

It is good practice in paperback drawn-on binding to score covers four times: twice for spine folds, and twice to form a 4mm hinge at front and back which adheres to the front and back pages.

Perforating

Perforating can be done either on the printing machine; or more normally, on a separate machine as part of the print-finishing process in much the same way as scoring (see above). Where perforating is done on the printing machine, a *perforating-strip* is fixed to the impression cylinder, and this punches the stock at the same time as the job is printed. It also destroys the blanket; so on-machine perforation is only for consideration where a print-run is long enough to absorb this extra cost.

Cutting/ trimming

Guillotines for cutting range from small hand-operated machines to large format fully-automatic and fully-programmable models. The guillotine operator achieves cutting position by knocking-up the stock to be trimmed to *back gauges* and *side gauges*. Guillotines can have airbeds to assist the operator in manoeuvring stocks of sheets; they can also have sophisticated programming capabilities with which the operator can preset the automatic positioning of the back gauges and side gauges for a whole sequence of cuts.

In magazine, book and similar applications, in-line three-knife trimmer is often used to cut the work to correct size in-line with the gatherer-stitcher.

In checking cutting quality, note that creased, feathered or torn edges can often be traced to a blunt guillotine blade.

Index cutting

This is the cutting out of a pre-printed leaf or series of leaves to indicate divisions in directory work, manuals, etc. Note the various sorts of index in use:

Stepped indexing

Cut steps of progressive length are made to the right-hand edge of each leaf; in alphabetical indexing, letter A takes most out of the leaf, letter Z the least.

Thumb indexing

Semi-circular thumb-shaped recesses are cut out in the leaves relevant to each division or referenced letter or article, etc. (expensive dictionaries, Bibles). Traditionally done by hand which was very costly, there are now machines available which automate the operation.

Tabbed indexing

Protruding pre-printed tabs are affixed in stepped progression down the sides of the appropriate leaves (loose-leaf books, etc.).

Banding

The securing of sets of loose-leaves, cards, etc. with a gummed paper band. Often used for loose-leaf refills, sets of envelopes, etc.

Loose-leaf insertion

Loose-leaf or ring-binders are available in a variety of pre-made formats with various sizes, shapes and configurations of ring. Print-finishing companies will normally purchase to the customer's order on his behalf, and insert the printed material as necessary. Silk-screen printing the covers of such binders can be an effective way of producing any titling necessary.

Padding

Padding is a cheap form of binding used for writing-paper pads, ruled pads, tear-off stationery, etc. The trimmed leaves are glued together along one edge with a single thin layer of PVA or other adhesive, which holds them together in a pad but allows each leaf to be torn away without tearing the paper. A strip of cotton or plastic is sometimes added for extra durability.

Counting

Finished items should be counted out - by hand or by machine – before packing according to the customer's order. Paper tabs, paper bands, or coloured paper dividers are useful in dividing stocks into convenient sub-divisions (25s, 50s, etc.).

8

Varnishing and laminating

Varnishing

Varnishing is normally performed by running the printed sheets through rollers. Special care needs to be taken with drying. Hence the introduction of accelerated infrared and ultraviolet drying. The common grades of varnish are as follows.

Machine varnish

Printed on the conventional litho printing machine: originally the result was a thin and hence low-gloss, low-resistant varnished finish, at worst barely noticeable except as a slight sheen on the finished product. However, the technology has since improved significantly.

Catalyst varnish

Applied on a separate roller-coating machine. A middle-of-the-road finish, with average resistance and reflectance. Normally dried by passing the varnished sheets through a gas drying oven.

NC varnish

A high-gloss, nitrocellulose varnish giving good protection and reasonable gloss. Called *liquid lamination* in the USA.

UV varnish

Installed in-line with a printing machine, a UV varnish unit deposits a high-gloss varnish which is dried by constant exposure to UV light.

UV varnish formulations are cured instantly by ultra-violet radiation after application of the varnish by roller-coating. A two or three roll coating head directly on to the sheet surface will be employed. A second coating head may be used to apply two layers of varnish, wet on wet, to give a very smooth, glossy finish.

Note that varnish offers scuff resistance and gloss, but in contrast to lamination, adds no extra *strength* to the substrate. Printing inks must be chosen which are suitable for the type of varnish which is to be used.

In considering the use of film lamination or UV varnishing to enhance printed or other work, there are a number of technical factors that should be taken into account in the selection and processing of materials for the job. These are:

☐ sheet size – maximum and minimum
☐ sheet allowances – margins and sheet layouts
☐ quantity allowances
☐ paper and board quality for best results
☐ use of anti-setoff spray
☐ ink formulation
☐ proofing.

Film lamination involves the application of liquid adhesive to the chosen film, which is dried before lamination. Solvent and water-based adhesives may be used depending on the film type and the requirements of the finished laminate.

The solvent or water is removed from the adhesive by heating the film web and directing hot air at the adhesive layer. This causes evaporation of the solvent and the adhesive becomes tacky, ready to be laminated to the surface of the print. The adhesive coated film and substrate are brought together at a heated nip, under high pressure, to ensure perfect contact with the printed surface. The adhesive then cures over a set period to give a permanent, indestructible bond between film and substrate surface.

Guillotining, creasing and embossing of laminated sheets too soon after lamination may lead to delamination or lift of film from the substrate. It is recommended that laminates be left for 24 hours prior to further processing. For high speed processing of long run work, the newer UV lamination process may be used. A UV radiation activated adhesive is cured by exposure to UV light passing through the laminating film after nipping to the substrate.

After 'reel' laminating a continuous web of film and substrate is brought together.

Laminating

Sheet allowances

When 'sheet' laminating, sheets are overlapped slightly to act as a continuous web when they meet the film web and are subsequently separated back into individual sheets for further sheetfed processing.

For sheetfed lamination, the film runs off one edge. The remaining three edges are free of film, two of which are for gripper edge and sidelay, which are 'clean' for any subsequent processing. Sheets are overlapped prior to lamination so there may be a slight indentation along the overlap line at the back of the sheet. To ensure that this falls outside the final working areas of the sheet, it is recommended that the following sheet format is always used.

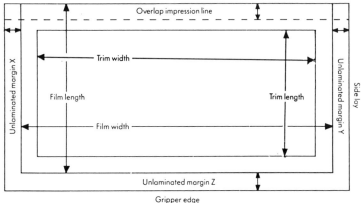

Sheets for film lamination are overlapped to form a web. The sheet that is overlapped has no film in the overlap area.

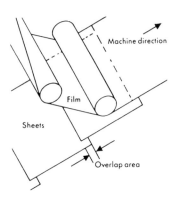

For reel lamination at least 5 mm is required on the x and y margins, so the maximum width of lamination coverage is 10mm less than the full width of the web.

To help the film laminator, always include a marked-up sheet with your order to show the area to be laminated, the finished trimmed size and gripper and sidelay edges. As a general guide allow an extra 7 mm of paper over and above the final trimmed size.

For roller-coat applied UV varnishes no grip edge is required as the sheet is completely covered with varnish. The grip and lay edge are left intact for subsequent processing.

Quantity allowances

It should be remembered that additional sheets will be required by the laminator/UV varnisher to set up his equipment prior to commencing the full production run. Typical numbers of overs required could be:

Number of sheets	*Number of overs*
Up to 5,000	5%
Over 5,000 sheets	3%
Over 100,000 sheets	1%

However, overs can vary according to the equipment used so it is worth checking with the finisher or printer.

Paper and board quality

For film lamination, most kinds and calipers of paper and board can be laminated or varnished if supplied flat and at a stable moisture content (relative humidity 50% to 55%). However, the quality of substrate chosen will have a bearing on the quality of the final finish. So whenever possible, and always where pre-grained, very rough or absorbent boards are selected, a proof is advised. It should be noted that the rougher matt coated artboards are not suitable for film lamination where a high quality finish is required.

The quality of a UV varnished surface will be more dependent on the board's or paper's smoothness and absorbency than that of a corresponding laminated finish. Paper and board for varnishing should have good varnish holdout, (surface oil absorbency test (SOAT) in excess of 60 seconds). Greater care in selecting board and paper for varnishing is recommended.

Use of anti-setoff spray

Excessive use of anti-setoff spray in any area of the printed sheet will be highlighted by lamination, causing a silvery appearance. In the case of varnishing, too much anti-setoff spray will prevent good varnish laydown and result in a poor finish. To achieve the best results, the minimum amount of finest grain spray and even application should be ensured.

Even better results can be obtained by printing with UV cured inks or with an emulsion coating in place of anti-setoff spray. The emulsion coating should be carefully chosen after discussion with the UV varnisher.

Ink formulations

Ink choice should be made in relation to the type of finish that is to be applied to the print. Inks used should be specified by the ink supplier's technicians or literature as suitable for laminating or varnishing. This means that the ink should have the following general characteristics.

☐ quick drying capability on the chosen substrate and with low residual solvent content
☐ have minimal content of wax, polythene, silicone and other surface acting agents. These are added to inks to give slip and prevent scuffing; qualities that the finish will impart itself
☐ should be tintorially strong so that ink application may be minimized along with the use of anti-setoff spray
☐ with solvent-based finishes, pigments should be resistant to solvents as defined by British Standard/BS4342 (Test method 4)
☐ UV inks should be applied to achieve a smooth finish that is completely thoroughly

8

cured and well adhered to the paper surface

☐ metallic inks can suffer from two unpredictable problems when laminated or UV varnished:

    ☐ immigration of lubricants to the ink's surface which prevents adhesion of laminating adhesives or causes reticulation of varnishes

    ☐ poor cohesive bonding between the flakes of metal in the ink which causes delamination of laminates, poor scratch resistance of varnishes and generally poor performance of most finishes.

It is recommended that metallic inks should not be used for any work which is to be subsequently laminated, or UV varnished.

Where sheets are to be foil stamped before finishing it is recommended that advice is sought from the laminator/varnisher, prior to stamping.

Proofing

Proofing is recommended where exact colour matching is required as lamination and UV varnishing may alter the optical qualities of an ink's surface to produce an apparent colour shift by highlighting the colour value of the ink pigment.

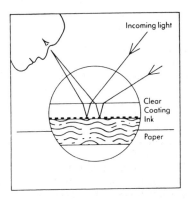

8

General binding

There are two main options with general binding (as opposed to bookbinding).

☐ saddle wire-stitching (usually referred to simply as *saddle-stitching*)
☐ perfect binding (sometimes called *cut-back binding*, *unsewn binding* or *thermoplastic binding*).

Other less common options are:

☐ saddle thread-sewing
☐ section sewing
☐ side wire-stabbing/side-sewing
☐ mechanical binding (wire-o, spiral, etc.).

Saddle-stitching

After printing, *folding* operations proceed as described elsewhere.

Gathering operations follow folding. When handling medium to long runs, gathering, saddle-stitching and trimming are often done in-line on a 'gatherer-stitcher'. The sequence of operations is as follows:

☐ *Gathering:* the sections are fed one over the next on a 'saddle' in the shape of an inverted V. The cover is folded either on-machine or off-machine and is fed on last.
☐ *Stitching:* the inset sections with their cover are stitched through the spine at the stitching unit. This may be a fully automatic or semi-automatic process.
☐ *Trimming:* an in-line guillotine unit or 'three-knife-trimmer', cuts the stitched books at head, fore-edge and tail to final size. Some in-line trimmers work copy-by-copy, others allow a pile of copies to build up before executing the final trim.

Saddle-stitching is the cheapest form of binding, but note the following constraints:

☐ There is a physical limit to the thickness which can be effectively stitched. With standard 85g/m^2 MF paper, for example, extents of more than 128pp can be difficult to stitch, and bulging at the spine can be unacceptably wide. In marginal circumstances it may be prudent to see a dummy before proceeding with the run. The imposition of the 'outset' pages in longer extent work should take into account the need for a wider back margin to allow for such bulging.

☐ Although it is a very secure form of binding, saddle-stitching will not allow a larger-extent magazine to lie flat when opened unless the pages are creased down by the reader. If this is an important consideration, an alternative binding method might be preferable.

☐ Stainless steel stitches are normally supplied as a matter of course. Where a part of the run is destined for overseas countries with high humidity, however, it is always wise to verify this point in order to be sure that rusting will not occur over a period of time.

After printing, *folding* operations proceed as described elsewhere.

Gathering operations follow folding. The gathering finishes with gathered but unbound copies, which are passed forward either on-line or off-line for binding.

The perfect binding process follows this sequence:

☐ the gathered sections are compressed and fed into the perfect-binder spine downwards in a continuous chain

☐ the bottom 3mm of each of the sets of gathered sections is milled off and roughened

☐ either one or two applications of adhesive are applied to the roughened spine edges

☐ the covers are scored and fed in and affixed to the glued spines fractionally after the adhesive

☐ the adhesive is dried/cured by heat or by other means.

The finished product is then trimmed, often in-line to the perfect-binding process, and stacked for packing and despatch.

Perfect binding

Perfect binding is more expensive than saddle wire-stitching, but has these principal advantages:

☐ a greater thickness can be bound in this way

☐ the finished product has a spine on which its title can be printed, as opposed to the saddle-stitched product which does not

☐ a perfect-bound product is generally perceived by the buyer as more substantial and better value than a saddle-stitched one.

The following considerations are important in deciding suitability for perfect binding:

☐ Whenever possible long grain direction of the paper should be used so as to avoid cocking of the page edges and enable better adhesion of the pages.

☐ The more fibrous and rough the surface, the better the paper will be for the process. Bulky newsprint is thus ideal; glossy artpaper is the least satisfactory. Standard MF or matt-coated cartridge papers are normally all right, but always need checking before the results can be guaranteed.

☐ Everything depends on the sorts and quality of adhesives being used. For extra security (or with difficult stocks) 'two-shot' binding is preferable: the first application is normally of cold-set PVA adhesive, the second of 'hot melt' thermoplastic material. 'One-shot' binding is adequate for more fibrous stock, and will normally be a hot-melt adhesive only.

☐ Note that the process is slower and requires much more quality control than saddle-stitching. As well as costing more it can take longer to do, and where publication speed is all important, the slower production speed may need to be taken into account.

Other techniques

The less common binding options include the following.

8

Saddle thread-sewing (singer sewing)

All the processes are as for saddle wire-stitching, except that the inset sections are thread-sewn through the backs rather than wire-stitched. Occasionally preferred for young children's magazines.

Section sewing

All the processes are as for perfect binding, except that the sections are sewn rather than thermoplastic bound. The principal applications are for shorter runs where durability is important or perhaps where artpaper makes perfect binding a less secure option (scientific or medical journals, etc.). It is also preferable for magazines or journals which will eventually be made up into cased bound volumes.

Side wire-stabbing

Is still used occasionally where permanence and security are required at relatively low expense. The gathered sections are stabbed through the side, near the spine, and the staples are covered by the hinge in the printed covers. Note that this can be a convenient binding method where many different kinds of stock, inset, etc. are involved. Side wire-stabbing will secure everything in place. Its main disadvantage is that the product does not open well, and does not lie flat when opened, except when forced to do so by creasing the pages near the spine.

Side-sewing (McCain sewing or Moffat sewing)

As in side wire-stabbing, the sections are laid on their side but are sewn through the side near the spine rather than wire-stabbed. A very secure and solid form of binding, which is mainly used for children's magazine work (and for children's books) particularly in the USA.

Mechanical binding

Comb or spiral bindings are particularly appropriate where a main requirement – as in a technical manual or DIY periodical – is that the pages stay flat when opened.

The folded and gathered sections are guillotined at the folded spines; drills make a series of evenly spaced holes along the backs; and continuous wire is either threaded through like a screw, or a patent system such as 'Wire-o' is used which clamps pre-formed open loops together through the holes to complete the rings.

Mechanical binding tends to be slow and relatively expensive.

Bookbinding

Conventional production-line bookbinding is sometimes known as edition binding. Leather binderies or small, specialist hand binderies cater for more expensive or specialized bookbinding requirements.

The conventional bookbinding options are these:

☐ saddle-stitching
☐ limp binding: unsewn or sewn
☐ cased binding: unsewn or sewn.

Saddle-stitching

Saddle-stitching operations and applications in bookwork are much the same as in general work.

Note that whereas generally it is common practice to complete all the operations of gathering, saddle-stitching and trimming in-line, it is not uncommon in bookwork for each of these operations to be carried out individually on free-standing unlinked equipment.

Saddle-wire stitching is a common bookbinding specification for lower-extent school texts, children's books, handbooks, brochures, etc.

Saddle thread-sewing or singer-sewing, described under general binding, is an alternative, less common binding method more favoured on the European Continent than in the UK. The endpapers are frequently wrapped and sewn with the printed pages of the book rather than tipped on to the bookblock.

Either saddle-stitching method is normally used for limp or paperback binding where the staples/thread go through the cover as well as the text in order to secure the two together. Saddle-wire stitching, and particularly saddle thread-sewing, can also be specified in cased binding however: the main text is saddle-stitched/thread-sewn, endpapers are added to the stitched bookblock, and the whole is cased into a pre-made case in exactly the same way as for normal edition casing-in. Saddle thread-sewn cased children's books bound in this way are quite common on the European Continent and in the USA, but

Edition binding

Quality control

Quality control aspects to be aware of when proposing saddle-stitched binding are:

the constraints on the extent of book possible without bulging occurring at the spine

the fact that the book will not lie open without the reader creasing the pages

the specification of wire to be used where books are destined for humid conditions.

---

less so in the UK. Such bindings are alternatively called *singer-sewn cased.*

The major equipment manufacturers in this area include AM Graphics and Muller Martini.

Limp binding

Limp unsewn binding

Limp unsewn, or *perfect*, binding operations are very much the same as for general binding. The sequence of operations in brief is as follows:

☐ the printed text sheets are folded (on-press if web printing, as a separate operation if sheetfed)
☐ the folded sections are gathered on a gathering-machine or by hand
☐ the gathered sections are perfect bound with the covers scored and drawn on within the same operation
☐ the finished books are trimmed to size, on- or off-line, and stacked for packing and despatch.

Limp unsewn binding is the cheapest bookbinding option, and is used for a wide variety of paperback fiction and non-fiction in all book formats where durability is not the main criterion. As stated under general binding, the paper used and the adhesives to be employed are all-important in achieving a satisfactory job.

High-volume mass-market paperbacks are bound in this way, but to speed up the finishing process it is common practice to print and finish all copies 'two-up head-to-head'. The texts are thus printed two-up; covers are printed likewise; the two-up gathered sections are perfect-bound; and at the final stage the perfect bound bookblock is slit into two just before trimming to give two finished copies per bookblock.

The major equipment manufacturers include Muller Martini, AM Graphics and Kolbus.

Two variants on the simple perfect binding principle are sometimes used:

☐ burst binding
☐ notch binding (sometimes called *slotted* binding).

Quality control

Quality control in any form of limp unsewn binding should include checking the evenness of application of adhesive, and ensuring that the covers are drawn on square.

Note that a significant enhancement in quality can be made by specifying that the adhesive is applied to the bookblock in a strip 4mm or so wide to either side of the spine as well as on the spine itself, and that the cover is scored with corresponding lines 4mm to either side of the spine lines. When the cover is drawn on, a glued 4mm hinge is thus formed at the front and back, which gives the binding extra strength at no extra cost.

Burst binding is normally associated with web printing. A series of bursts are made at the folding stage along the section folds; the gathered sections are fed through a perfect-binding machine but without the spine-milling unit being engaged; and the bursts in the backs permit adhesive from the perfect-binding machine to penetrate through and secure the leaves. The resulting binding gives a stronger result than the simple perfect-bound process in which the spines are milled away.

Notch binding is associated with sheetfed printing. It is similar in concept to burst binding, except that slots or notches, rather than bursts, are made in the folded sections at each spine, and they are made by a series of *notching-wheels* on the sheet folding machine rather than by punches on the folding unit of the printing machine. Adhesive binding then proceeds on the same principle as for burst binding, with the same enhanced results claimed.

It should be noted that wraps or inserts are out of the question in the burst or notch binding styles because there can be no guarantee that the apertures in the spines of the wrapped sections will line up.

Limp sewn binding

The most common specification is section-sewn continuous, with the cover drawn on to the sewn bookblock. The main operations are the same as for limp unsewn binding, above, with the exception that the sections are sewn together rather than milled away at the spine before the covers are drawn on. The 'drawing-on' operation is often performed on a perfect-binding machine in which the milling unit has been disconnected.

The main object in section-sewing a limp book is normally to achieve extra security in the binding. Factors which will influence this choice should be:

☐ where the paper is matt coated or gloss art
☐ where the extent of the book is particularly long
☐ where the book will have frequent handling (as in works of reference, dictionaries, etc.)
☐ where the period of use will be over many years.

Note too that books with illustrations laid over double-page spreads will normally indicate sewn binding (or special imposition for unsewn binding). Sewn binding also helps a book lie flat when opened; unsewn books will tend to resist opening wide, and can only be opened flat by creasing the pages down, or wrenching the book open and jeopardizing the glued binding.

Section-sewing is always more secure than perfect-binding, but is correspondingly more expensive.

Thread-sealing is a binding technique which combines features of both sewing and adhesive binding. Each individual section is thread-sealed as it is folded with a couple of thread stitches through its folded spine; and each section so secured is then glued to the section either side of it in much the same way as is done for burst- or notch-binding (see above). No thread runs from one section to another as in standard section-sewing.

This method offers economies over normal section-sewing costs because once thread-sealed, the individual sections can be gathered, covered and trimmed in-line (whereas standard section-sewing involves separating the gathering stage from the covering/trimming stage, and is much slower).

Side-sewing, in which the sections are laid on their side and sewn through the side near the spine (rather than being sewn through the spines of each section and linked together as with section-sewn continuous) is a particularly strong specification much favoured in the USA for children's and reference books which are likely to undergo a lot of wear and tear. It is practically indestructible, but can give a 'mouse-trap' effect if specified on books with stiff, unyielding paper.

Cased binding

Edition cased binding – as described here – imitates the true 'bound' book in appearance but not in structure. The true 'bound' book has the boards attached to the body of the book; the cased book has the hard case made apart from the book and assembled with the text only at the final stage.

Cased binding can be either sewn or unsewn, and as with limp binding the options within each are:

☐ unsewn: perfect bound, burst bound, notch-bound

☐ sewn: section-sewn continuous, thread-sealed, side-sewn.

Sequence of events

Conventional section-sewn cased binding is the most common specification, and these are the operations:

1. The printed sheets off machine are folded to a predetermined imposition

2. The folded sections are bundled

3. The first and last sections in the book are separated out and have the endpapers tipped-on either by hand or machine; or endpapering may be carried out on the binding line itself

4. The sections are gathered on a gathering machine into book order

5. The gathered sections are collated

6. The collated sections are threadsewn on either semi-automatic or automatic sewing machines. The standard section-alongside-section sewing method is known as *French sewing, continuous sewing*, or *section-sewing*, to differentiate it from inset singer-sewing and from side-sewing

7. The books are divided off according to the collation marks: at this stage they are called *book-blocks.*

8. Each book-block is forwarded on for final back-lining and then casing-in using either in-line equipment or freestanding equipment; and generally following this pattern of operations:

(a) *nipping (crushing, smashing)* to remove air from the sections

(b) a light coating of glue over the sewn backs to secure the sewing threads

(c) a three-knife trim, to give correctly trimmed blocks

(d) *rounding and backing*, to put a 'round' into the shape of the book-block and a joint below the shoulder. The name of this operation is often abbreviated to *r&b* (rounding and backing), or *r&j* (rounding and jointing). Rounding is performed by rollers, and the backing (or jointing) is carried out by 'irons' of various widths

(e) first and second linings are applied to the glued and sewn spines: the first lining of expandable mull, and the second of stout kraft paper as a stiffener

(f) head and tailbands are added if specified

(g) casing-in: the endpapers are glued up and the book-blocks are fed inside the pre-formed cases and pressed

(h) the cased books are jacketed either by hand or using a jacketing machine.

Cases are made apart on a case-making machine, which is set up to affix the pre-cut binder's boards to the chosen covering material in the prescribed positions for the size of the book. The pre-made case is most normally blocked using a copper or zinc binder's *brass* (*die*), which using heat and pressure impresses imitation gold or silver foil into the case to form the lettering. The blocked case is affixed to the endpapers to complete binding at stage 8(g) above.

Thread-sealing techniques when used in edition cased binding replace the conventional section-sewing process at stage 6 by thread-sealing each section in-line with folding at stage 1. Stages 7, 8(a), 8(b) and 8(e) are then omitted.

Side-sewing techniques can be used to replace the conventional section-sewing process (stage 6) when extra durability is required. This specification is uncommon (and expensive) in the UK and Europe, but much more current in the USA.

Unsewn edition cased binding follows the same general principles described above, with the exception that instead of being sewn, the book-block is perfect-bound and backlined using a flexible mull lining at stage 6; and stages 7, 8(a), 8(b) and 8(e) are omitted.

Burst-binding and notch-binding techniques are also used in cased binding. At stage 6, the burst or notched book-blocks are adhesive bound and lined and again stages 7, 8(a), 8(b) and 8(e) are omitted.

A number of linked systems are available which bring in line all the later stages of bookbinding (as in 8 above). Kolbus and Stahl-VBF flow lines are probably the most used of these.

Materials

A *covering* is the name given to the material used in making the case of a hardback book. The coverings used in the large majority of edition cased books are dyed, embossed and reinforced paper rather than cloth. In roughly ascending order of cost/durability, the options are as follows.

Non-woven materials (paper, or plastic coated paper):

☐ plain fibrefelts: dyed embossed and reinforced papers, from 105g/m² upwards

☐ over-printed fibrefelts: similar base paper but in heavier weights up to 155g/m²

☐ pyroxilin-coated fibrefelts: reinforced and lightly plasticized papers

☐ over-printed pyroxilin-coated fibrefelts: ditto, with over-printed patterns

☐ vinyl-coated papers: papers with a tearproof, washproof surface

☐ plastic-coated fibres: heavy duty, embossed, 'imitation leather' finish.

Woven materials (starch-filled or nitrocellulose-filled woven cloth):

☐ 'whiteback' cloth: cotton filled with starch, dyed and coated on one side only, calendered

☐ leather-cloth: plasticated cotton, dyed-through, calendered

☐ art canvas: loose wove, strong cotton with a tissue lining

☐ buckram: heavy duty, stiff, dyed-through and coated cotton-base.

Leathers:

☐ goathides
☐ pigskins

☐ calfskins
☐ vellum
☐ sheepskin
☐ forels
☐ reconstituted leather.

Production runs in these materials are rare.

Most non-woven and woven materials are supplied in 100 metre rolls of approximately one metre wide and charged per running metre. The more expensive non-woven materials are heavier in substance, have more expensive over-printing, and are coated with nitro-cellulose or other plastifiers to give surface protection and extra strength.

Woven materials cost more according to the fineness of the cotton weave, and the degree of dying, filling and coating applied to the base cloth. Note that man-made fibres, particularly rayon, are replacing cotton in some of the woven-cloth qualities, and provide a characteristically uniform, precise and even base surface for dying and coating.

Leathers are charged according to area and quality of hide. Expert advice is recommended when ordering leather.

The usual sorts of boards available for case-making are:

☐ chipboard: the cheapest sort of board, made from waste paper
☐ Eskaboard: a crossed-grain board, so designed to prevent warping
☐ millboard: waste-paper furnish with some flax or hemp for extra strength.

Boards are normally provided to one of the following specifications, listed here with approximate equivalents:

1700 microns 070" 1200gsm 24oz
(Crown, Large Crown 8vo)

2000 microns 080" 1400gsm 28oz
(Demy 8vo, Royal 8vo)

2300 microns 090" 1600gsm 32oz
(Quarto sizes)

Warping is the main risk associated with boards. While the risk can never be eliminated, the following precautions will minimize the risk:

☐ specify that all boards should be cut long grain (i.e. with the grain direction parallel to the head-to-tail dimension of the book)

☐ specify that the grain direction of the covering material must likewise be parallel to the spine; and also the endpapers, if possible.

☐ use the heaviest weight and best quality of board consistent with the budget

☐ allow boards time to mature both before production and afterwards in transit. Pack books in porous materials, not plastic, if manufacturing in a country with high humidity (e.g. the Far East) for sale in an area of less humidity (e.g. Europe).

Quality control

The following aspects of cased binding should be monitored:

☐ *Folding.* Check that the folding is square, and if it does not appear to be so, check the back-up and imposition of the printed sections.

☐ *Rounding and backing.* Rounding is often inadequately carried out on sewn work, and is notoriously difficult to do effectively with unsewn work.

☐ *Backlining.* Check the quality of linings used. Occasionally only one lining is used; this both weakens the backs of the sections, and allows the risk of glue seeping through and causing the backs to adhere to the case hollow.

☐ *Casemaking.* Check bubbling or smearing underneath the case material. Check the case hollow for strength.

☐ *Boards.* Take precautions against warping in more quality-conscious work.

☐ *Blocking.* Inaccurate application of heat or pressure can cause imperfect transfer of the foil to the material. Particularly rough or heavily embossed materials can benefit from a run of 'blind' blocking before foil blocking in order to ensure that the surface will accept the foil properly.

☐ *Casing-in and forming.* Check that the shoulders, grooves and hollows are properly formed. A square-back, shoulderless case should always be avoidable.

☐ *Jacketing.* Check that the jackets are trimmed correctly – 1 or 2mm less than the depth of the board prevents the risk of scuffing the jacket at top and bottom – and that jackets are wrapped around the books accurately.

☐ *Packing.* Cased books are best packed with spines turned alternately to left and right. This allows space for shoulders and joints.

8

Specialist bookbinding

Handbinding operations for short-run, expensive work (limited editions, etc.) include the following. Note that it is important to take specialist advice when specifying this style of work.

Folding

Often done by hand, using a bone folder to make especially sharp folds.

Sewing

Traditional hand-sewing might be specified as either 'on tapes' or 'on cords'. Such sewing is carried out at a sewing frame which carries the tapes or cords, and the pages of each section are sewn through and to each other incorporating the tapes/cords in the structure of the sewing. A handsewn book on tapes/cords is thus extremely durable.

Endpapering

Traditional endpapers in hand binding are made extra-strong by using a double-fold sheet reinforced with cloth, which is sewn in with the main book-block, instead of being merely strip glued as in edition cased binding. Marbled endpapers are often used.

Forwarding

A typical sequence of operations might be:

☐ trimming the book-block

☐ gilding or edge-colouring; gilding can be done either with real or imitation gold, by hand or machine

☐ edge-colouring can be done either by application of a dye with a sponge, or by spray

☐ rounding: done by hand, with a hammer

☐ backing, or jointing, again done by hand, with a hammer and a range of special tools

☐ backlining; specially strong mulls and kraft papers are used.

8

Casemaking

The case is attached to the book-block not just by the endpaper-glueing process, but by securing the boards themselves to the book-block using the ends of the tapes/cords. In the case of cords, the boards are drilled and the cords are laced into the holes. In the case of tapes, a split or 'made' board is used: the board is slit through for about one-third of its width, and the tapes are secured inside the slit.

Covering

A typical covering might be leather or partial leather.

The leathers most frequently used in bookbinding are as follows:

☐ *goatskin:* probably the most commonly used leather, otherwise called morocco; Niger Morocco (Nigerian goat), Turkish goat crushed levant and ordinary levant are the more usual qualities

☐ *pigskin:* of great durability, but very stiff and inflexible, so suitable only for large, heavy books

☐ *calf:* less durable than either goatskin or pigskin, but has a naturally smooth surface and great flexibility

☐ *vellum* made from the inside of calfskin; a beautiful surface, but difficult to handle, expensive and rather difficult to tool

☐ *sheepskin:* soft and smooth-surfaced, with reasonable durability

☐ *forels:* split sheepskin, less expensive and less durable

☐ *reconstituted leather* is also available at the cheaper end of the range.

Finishings

Finishings are elaborate hand-tooled and decorative effects achieved by using onlays or inlays of skivers – thinly pared leathers – in contrasting colours, and gold or coloured decorations impressed into the surface of the leather with special hand tools.

Quarter-bound and half-bound binding styles are commonly adopted. In the quarter-bound style, the spine is covered in one material (often leather) while the sides are covered in another (often cloth or marbled paper). The half-bound style adds to this specification with leather edges at the top and bottom corners of the book.

Note that the methods and costs involved in true hand-binding bear no relationship at all to the method and cost structure for conventional flow-line edition binding, and true hand-binding is normally viable only for single or low-quantity presentation copies, prestige monographs, specialist limited editions, etc.

Certain categories of work combine both flow-line methods and hand methods, notably *bible-binding* and *account-book binding*. In these cases, folding and sewing might well be conventional: but extra strength and attractiveness is brought to the binding by (for example) edge-gilding, the use of marbled endpapers, and an attractively blocked, leather-covered binding case. The cost structure here will depend upon the quality of materials specified and the proportion of hand to 'edition' work, but it may well be viable for production quantities where a high selling price can be obtained.

9 General reference

Reference tables

Metric weights and measures

Length	10 ångström	=1 nanometre
	1000 nanometres	=1 micrometre
	1000 micrometres	=1 millimetre
	10 millimetres	=1 centimetre
	10 centimetres	=1 decimetre
	10 decimetres	=1 metre
	10 metres	=1 dekametre
	10 dekametres	=1 hectometre
	10 hectometres	=1 kilometre
	1000 kilometres	=1 megametre
Weight	1000 milligrams	=1 gram
	10 grams	=1 dekagram
	10 dekagrams	=1 hectogram
	10 hectograms	=1 kilogram
	100 kilograms	=1 quintal
	10 quintals	=1 tonne
Area	100 sq millimetres	=1 sq centimetre
	100 sq centimetres	=1 sq decimetre
	100 sq decimetres	=1 sq metre
	100 sq metres	=1 are
	100 ares	=1 hectare
	100 hectares	=1 sq kilometre
Capacity	10 millilitres	=1 centilitre
	10 centilitres	=1 decilitre
	10 decilitres	=1 litre
	10 litres	=1 dekalitre
	10 dekalitres	=1 hectolitre
	10 hectolitres	=1 kilolitre
Volume	1000 cu millimetres	=1 cu centimetre
	1000 cu centimetres	=1 cu decimetre
	1000 cu decimetres	=1 cu metre
	1000 cu metres	=1 cu dekametre
	1000 cu dekametres	=1 cu hectometre

Imperial weights and measures (UK)

Length		
	12 inches	=1 foot
	3 feet	=1 yard
	22 yards	=1 chain
	10 chains	=1 furlong
	220 yards	=1 furlong
	8 furlongs	=1 mile
	1760 yards	=1 mile
	5280 feet	=1 mile
Weight	16 ounces	=1 pound
	14 pounds	=1 stone
	2 stones	=1 quarter
	28 pounds	=1 quarter
	4 quarters	=1 hundredweight
	8 stones	=1 hundredweight
	20 hundredweights	=1 ton
	2240 pounds	=1 ton
Area	144 sq inches	=1 sq foot
	4840 sq yards	=1 acre
	640 acres	=1 sq mile
Capacity	8 fluid drachms	=1 fluid ounce
	5 fluid ounces	=1 gill
	4 gills	=1 pint
	2 pints	=1 quart
	4 quarts	=1 gallon
	2 gallons	=1 peck
	4 pecks	=1 bushel
	8 bushels	=1 quarter
	36 gallons	=1 bulk barrel
Volume	1728 cu inches	=1 cu foot
	27 cu feet	=1 cu yard
	5.8 cu feet	=1 bulk barrel
	100 cu feet	=1 register ton
		(*Shipping*)

(The first entry under Length is labelled Length *in italics.)*

Metric multiples

Symbol	Prefix	Multiplication factor
p	pico	0.000000000001
n	nano	0.000000001
μ	micro	0.000001
m	milli	0.001
c	centi	0.01
d	deci	0.1
-	-	-
da	deka (or deca)	10
h	hecto	100
k	kilo	1000
my	myria	10000
M	mega	1000000
G	giga	1000000000
T	tera	1000000000000

Conversion Imperial-metric

	Imperial	Multiplication factor	Metric
Length	inches	2.54000	centimetres
	feet	0.3048	metres
	yards	0.9144	metres
	miles	1.609344	kilometres
Weight	ounces	28.3495	grams
	pounds	0.45359	kilograms
	short tons (2000 lbs)	0.907185	tonnes
	long tons (2240 lbs)	1.01605	tonnes
Area	sq inches	6.4516	sq centimetres
	sq feet	0.092903	sq metres
	sq yards	0.836127	sq metres
	sq miles	2.58999	sq kilometres
	acres	0.404686	hectares
Capacity & Vol	cu inches	16.387064	cu centimetres
	pints	0.5683	litres
	gallons	4.546	litres
Velocity	miles per hour	1.609344	kilometres per hr
	feet per second	0.3048	metres per second
Temperature	degrees Fahrenheit	$(-32)x^5/_9$	degrees Celsius

Conversion Metric-Imperial

	Metric unit	Multiplication factor	Imperial
Length	centimetres	0.3937	inches
	metres	3.2808	feet
	metres	1.0936143	yards
	kilometres	0.62137	miles
Weight	grams	0.03527	ounces
	kilograms	2.20462	pounds
	tonnes	1.10231	short tons
	tonnes	0.984207	long tons
Area	sq centimetres	0.155	sq inches
	sq metres	10.7639	sq feet
	sq metres	1.9599	sq yards
	sq kilometres	0.3861	sq miles
	hectares	2.47101	acres
Capacity and Vol	cu centimetres	0.06102	cu inches
	litres	1.7598	pints
	litres	0.2200	gallons
Velocity	kilometres p. hour	0.62137	miles per hour
	metres per second	3.2808	feet per second
Temperature	degrees Celsius	$x^9/_5(+32)$	degrees F

Typographical measurements

Points and Picas (Anglo-American standard)

	Inches	Millimetres
Anglo-American point	.013837	0.351
Pica	.166044	4.218

Didots and Ciceros (European standard)

Didot point	.0148	0.376
Cicero	.1776	4.511

Conversion Factor Picas to Ciceros

1.069596 (1.0696)

Conversion Factor Ciceros to Picas

0.9349324 (0.9349)

Conversion tables Anglo-American and Didot

	Anglo-American	
Point size	*Inches*	*Millimetres*
1	.013837	.351
3	.041511	1.054
6	.083022	2.109
7	.096859	2.460
8	.110696	2.812
9	.124533	3.163
10	.138370	3.515
11	.152207	3.866
12	.166044	4.218
14	.193718	4.920
18	.249066	6.326
24	.332088	8.435

	Didot	
Point size	*Inches*	*Millimetres*
1	.0148	.376
3	.0444	1.128
6	.0888	2.256
7	.1036	2.631
8	.1184	3.007
9	.1332	3.383
10	.1480	3.759
11	.1628	4.135
12	.1776	4.511
14	.2072	5.263
18	.2664	6.767
24	.3552	9.022

Screen rulings

Lines per inch	*Nearest standard equivalent lines per cm*	*Paper surface*
65	26	newsprint
85	34	newsprint
100	40	MF
120	48	MF/matt coated
133	54	MF/matt coated/art
150	60	matt coated/art
175	70	art
200	80	art

Paper sizes

Stock sizes for normal trim work

Sheet size	Millimetres	Equivalent in inches	A4 pages to view	A4 pages from sheet
RA0	860x1220	$33^7/_4$x48	16	32
RA1	610x 860	24 x$33^7/_8$	8	16
RA2	430x 610	$16^7/_8$x24	4	8

Stock sizes for bleed trim work

Sheet size	Millimetres	Equivalent in inches	A4 pages to view	A4 pages from sheet
SRA0	900x1280	$35^3/_8$x$50^3/_8$	16	32
SRA1	640x900	$25^1/_4$x$35^3/_8$	8	16
SR2	450x640	$17^3/_4$x$25^1/_4$	4	8

Book sheet sizes (quad sheets)

	Metric		*Imperial*	
	mm	*inches*	*mm*	*inches*
Crown	768x1008	$30^1/_4$x$39^5/_8$	762x1016	30x40
Large crown	816x1056	$32^1/_8$x$41^5/_8$	813x1067	32x42
Demy	888x1128	35x$44^3/_8$	889x1143	35x45
Royal	960x1272	$37^3/_4$x$50^1/_8$	1016x1270	40x50
Foolscap			686x864	27x34
Large Post			838x1067	33x42
Medium			914x1168	36x46
Imperial			1118x1524	44x60

A series sheet sizes

Sheet size	Millimetres	Equivalent in inches
4A	1682x2378	$66\frac{1}{4}$x$93\frac{5}{8}$
2A	1189x1682	$46\frac{5}{8}$x$66\frac{1}{4}$
A0	841x1189	$33\frac{1}{8}$x$46\frac{5}{8}$
A1	594x841	$23\frac{5}{8}$x$33\frac{1}{8}$
A2	420x594	$16\frac{1}{2}$x$23\frac{5}{8}$
A3	297x420	$11\frac{5}{8}$x$16\frac{1}{2}$
A4	210x297	$8\frac{1}{4}$x$11\frac{3}{4}$
A5	148x210	$5\frac{7}{8}$x$8\frac{1}{4}$
A6	105x148	$4\frac{1}{8}$x$5\frac{7}{8}$
A7	74x105	$2\frac{7}{8}$x$4\frac{1}{8}$
A8	52x74	2x$2\frac{7}{8}$
A9	37x52	$1\frac{1}{2}$x2
A10	26x37	1x$1\frac{1}{2}$

B series for posters

Sheet size	Millimetres	Equivalent in inches
4B	2000x2828	$78\frac{3}{4}$x$111\frac{3}{8}$
2B	1414x2000	$55\frac{5}{8}$x$78\frac{3}{4}$
B0	1000x1414	$39\frac{3}{8}$x$55\frac{5}{8}$
B1	707x1000	$27\frac{7}{8}$x$39\frac{3}{8}$
B2	500x707	$19\frac{5}{8}$x$27\frac{7}{8}$
B3	353x500	$3\frac{7}{8}$x$19\frac{5}{8}$
B4	250x353	$9\frac{7}{8}$x$13\frac{7}{8}$
B5	176x250	7x$9\frac{7}{8}$

C series for envelopes

	Millimetres	Equivalent in inches	Common use
C0	917x1297	$36\frac{1}{8}$x51	
C1	648x917	$25\frac{1}{2}$x$36\frac{1}{8}$	
C2	458x648	18x$25\frac{1}{2}$	
C3	324x458	$12\frac{3}{4}$x18	
C4	229x324	9x$12\frac{3}{4}$	takes A4 sheet flat
C5	162x229	$6\frac{3}{8}$x9	takes A5 sheet flat
C6	114x162	$4\frac{1}{2}$x$6\frac{3}{8}$	takes A5 folded once
C7/6	81x162	$3\frac{1}{4}$x$6\frac{3}{8}$	takes A5 folded twice
C7	81x114	$3\frac{1}{4}$x$4\frac{1}{2}$	
DL	110x220	$4\frac{3}{8}$x$8\frac{5}{8}$	takes A4 folded twice

American
basis weights

The basis size is the standard size in a given grade used to determine the basis weight. See Section 7 (Paper) for further explanation. This table shows common basis size weights by paper type.

Paper type	Basis weight	Basis size weights
Bond	17x22	13, 16, 20, 24, 28, 32, 36, 40
Uncoated book	25x38	30, 40, 45, 50, 55, 60, 65, 70, 75, 80, 90, 100, 120
Coated book	25x38	30, 40, 45, 50, 55, 60, 65, 70, 75, 80, 90, 100, 120
Text	25x38	90, 100, 120, 140, 160, 180
Cover	20x26	25, 35, 40, 50, 55, 60, 65, 80,

Book trimmed page sizes

Metric book sizes

	Trimmed 8vo		Trimmed 4to	
	mm	inches	mm	inches
Crown	186x123	$7\frac{1}{4}$x$4\frac{7}{8}$	246x189	$9\frac{3}{4}$x$7\frac{1}{2}$
Large crown	198x129	$7\frac{3}{4}$x$5\frac{1}{8}$	258x201	$10\frac{1}{8}$x$7\frac{7}{8}$
Demy	216x138	$8\frac{1}{2}$x$5\frac{3}{8}$	276x219	$10\frac{7}{8}$x$8\frac{5}{8}$
Royal	234x156	$9\frac{1}{4}$x$6\frac{1}{8}$	312x237	$12\frac{1}{4}$x$9\frac{3}{8}$

Imperial book sizes

	Trimmed 8vo		Trimmed 4to	
	mm	inches	mm	inches
Crown	184x124	$7\frac{1}{4}$x$4\frac{7}{8}$	248x187	$9\frac{3}{4}$x$7\frac{3}{8}$
Large crown	197x130	$7\frac{3}{4}$x$5\frac{1}{8}$	260x200	$10\frac{1}{4}$x$7\frac{7}{8}$
Demy	216x140	$8\frac{1}{2}$x$5\frac{1}{2}$	279x219	11x$8\frac{5}{8}$
Royal	248x156	$9\frac{3}{4}$x$6\frac{1}{8}$	311x251	$12\frac{1}{4}$x$9\frac{7}{8}$
Foolscap	165x105	$6\frac{1}{2}$x$4\frac{1}{8}$	210x168	$8\frac{1}{4}$x$6\frac{5}{8}$
Large post	203x130	8x$5\frac{1}{8}$	260x206	$10\frac{1}{4}$x$8\frac{1}{8}$
Medium	222x143	$8\frac{3}{4}$x$5\frac{5}{8}$	286x225	$11\frac{1}{4}$x$8\frac{7}{8}$
Imperial	273x187	$10\frac{3}{4}$x$7\frac{3}{8}$	375x276	$14\frac{3}{4}$x$10\frac{7}{8}$

A

A The **A series** is an international ISO range of paper sizes reducing from 4A at 1682 x 2378 through AO at 841 x 1189 to A10 at 26 x 37, with subsidiary RA and SRA sizes. Each size folds in half to preserve the same proportions of 1 : √2 at each reduction. See also **B, C.**

accordion fold Parallel folds in paper, opening like an accordion bellows, each in an opposite direction from the preceding fold.

acetate Transparent sheet of film fixed over camera-ready artwork used for positioning repro or for marking instructions.

achromatic colour An intermediate grey level in the monochromatic grey scale in computer graphics.

achromatic separations Colour separations produced by CCR (**complementary colour removal**). The black printer carries more detail than with conventional separations and the tertiary, or complementary, elements of any colour hue are removed. Also called **ICR (integrated colour removal)** or **GCR (grey component replacement).**

acid-free paper Generic term to describe paper which is free from acid-producing chemicals which reduce longevity.

additive primaries Red, green and blue, which when added together as light appear as white. Known also as the **light primaries.** Their complements or 'opposites' are known as the **light secondaries:** each one is made up of two colours out of the three, taken in turn. They are cyan (i.e. minus red), magenta (i.e. minus green), yellow (i.e. minus blue).

adhesive binding Binding style for books and magazines involving the application of a hot-melt adhesive to the roughened or ground back to hold the pages and cover together. Also called **cut-back binding, perfect binding, thermoplastic binding, threadless binding.**

advance sheets Folded and collated sheets for the publisher's approval before binding.

alcohol damping The use of alcohol in the **damping** solution in a litho press.

align To line up type, horizontally or vertically, using a typographical criterion, e.g. **base alignment** (q.v.).

alphanumeric Relating to the full alphabetic and numeric character set of a machine.

American Standard Code for Information Interchange Abbreviated to **ASCII.** A data transmission coding standard designed to achieve compatibility between data devices. Each symbol in ASCII code consists of 7 data bits and one **parity bit** for error-checking purposes. This combination allows for 128 code combinations. If the eighth bit is not used for parity checking, a total of 256 code combinations is possible.

anamorphic scaling Scaling in which one dimension of a subject is reduced / enlarged to a different proportion from the other dimension: for example, a half-tone reduced 30% across the width and retained at original size in the depth.

antique A printing paper with a rough finish but good printing surface valued in book printing for its high volume characteristics. Also called **antique wove.**

appearing size The physical size of a type, as opposed to its nominal point size. Two type faces of the same point size can have very different appearing sizes.

arabic figures The numerals 1,2,3,4, etc. as distinct from the Roman I, II, III, IV. Evolved from Arabic symbols. Arabic figures can be typeset as **lining** or **non-lining figures** (q.v.).

artboard Woodfree board coated to a high finish for fine printing of half-tones.

art paper Paper coated with china clay and polished to a high finish.

artwork Original illustrative copy or typesetting ready for reproduction at pre-film stage.

ascender The part of a lower case character which extends above the **x-height** (q.v.). As in b,d,f, etc. See also **descender, extenders.**

ASCII See American Standard Code for Information Interchange.

ASPIC Acronym for Authors' Symbolic Pre-press Interfacing Codes: the generic coding system endorsed by the BPIF.

assembly Bringing together pieces of film to make up rows of pages and produce final imposed foils for platemaking. Also called **planning** (q.v.).

author's corrections Corrections made by the author on proofs and changing the original copy as distinct from **printer's errors or literals** (q.v.) made by the typesetter. Author's corrections are by convention marked in blue; printer's errors or literals are marked in red.

automatic kerning or autokerning The ability of some photosetting output systems automatically to adjust the letter fit of certain character combinations in text so that spacing is kept visually even.

autopositive film Photographic material which produces a positive image from a positive original without an intermediate.

autoreversal film Type of film used for making contact film duplication without requiring an intermediate stage of negative or positive, i.e. will give a negative from a negative or positive from a positive. Also known as **direct-duplicating film.**

a/w See **artwork.**

B

B The **B series** is an international ISO range of sizes designed for large items (wallcharts, posters) and falling between the **A series** sizes (q.v.).

back 1. The binding edge of a book. The back margin is the space between the type and bound edge. 2. In binding, to form a shoulder on each side of the spine. See **backing, rounding and backing.**

backing In binding, the operations which form a shoulder on each side of the spine. Also known as **jointing** (q.v.). In paper the carrier sheet for a peel-off stock.

bad break Undesirable end-of-line hyphenation of a word.

band strapping Enclosing a stack of printed material with a strong, thin plastic band to secure it. The machine is a **band strapper**.

bank Grade of lightweight writing and printing paper used for correspondence, multi-part sets etc. Weights over 60gsm are known as **bonds** (q.v.).

bar code Symbol used for machine recognition such as those defined by the European Article Numbering System which represents the **ISBN** of a book presented in standardized machine-readable form, and appearing in a defined position on the outside of a publication for stock control purposes. Add-on features can include the encodation of price.

baryta Heavy grade of coated paper sometimes used for reproduction proofs.

base alignment Aligning characters of different sizes on the same line. See **base line, align.**

base line Horizontal line on which characters in a line of type appear to stand.

base paper Paper to which a coating is to be added. Also called **body paper** or **body stock.**

basic size American paper term for the specified sheet size used to define **basis weight** (q.v.). Different papers have different basic sizes: the basic size applied to book papers is 25" x 38".

basis weight or substance 1. The weight of a material, usually paper, defined in grams per square metre. 2.(USA) Weight in pounds per ream of paper cut to **basic size** (q.v.). Typical US weights for book papers are 50lbs (equivalent to 74gsm), 55lb (equivalent to 81gsm), 60lb (equivalent to 89gsm).

bed The flat metal part of a printing machine which holds the type form during printing.

Bible paper Very thin, strong, opaque printing paper used where low bulk, or weight, is needed. Originally made for Bibles and prayer books, also used for dictionaries and air mailed publications.

bimetal plate Lithographic plate where the printing image area base is usually brass or copper, and the non-printing area is usually aluminium, stainless steel or chromium. Used for long runs.

blad Sample pages of a book produced in the form of a booklet and used for promotional purposes.

blade coating Paper coating method where a surplus of coating is applied to the web and then levelled and controlled by a flexible steel blade.

blanket A rubber-surfaced sheet clamped around the cylinder of an offset litho printing press which transfers the printing image from plate to paper.

blanket-to-blanket Printing configuration where two blanket cylinders act as opposing impression cylinders printing both sides of the sheet or web simultaneously.

bleaching Part of paper-making process where chemical treatment is used to purify, whiten, brighten and improve permanence of the pulp.

bleach-out Underdeveloped bromide print used as a basis for a line drawing. The bromide print is bleached away after the drawing is finished.

bleed Printed matter running off the cut edge of a page. The bleed allowance beyond the **trimmed size** is usually 3mm to ensure a clean cut-off.

blind blocking Blocking or stamping of covers or jackets without metallic foil in order to smoothe down, indent, or emboss the surface. Also called **blind stamping.**

block 1. Etched copper or zinc plate used in binding for impressing or stamping a design on a cover. In letterpress, a plate which is mounted and printed with type. 2. Computer term for a group of bytes (q.v.) of information. 3. Any group of words or files treated as a unit.

blocking 1. Binding operation to impress a design or lettering into a book cover, often filling the impression with metal or pigment **foil**. 2. Fault where stack of printed sheets stick together as the ink dries.

blue key In film assembly, a form of key in which the image is produced photographically in drop-out blue, and is non-printing.

blueprints Contact dyeline proofs made on paper from film. Used for general checking purposes especially positioning. Also called **blues, bluelines, diazo prints, dyelines** and **ozalid prints.**

board General term for paper above 220gsm (although sometimes applied to substances down to 200gsm).

body copy or **body matter** Text pages as distinct from prelims, endmatter, index, etc.

body text The main text of a book.

bold Heavier version of a typeface, as distinct from light or medium. Sometimes abbreviated to **bf** (bold face).

bond Range of heavier substance printing and writing papers often used for letterheads, invoices, etc. Similar papers of lighter substance (under about 60gsm) are known as **banks** (q.v.).

book-block Book at the binding stage after sewing or perfect binding but before **forwarding** operations have been carried out.

book proof Page proofs paperback-bound in the form of the finished book.

BPIF British Printing Industries Federation.

brace Form of bracket { }, mainly used in tables.

brass A die made from metal and used for blocking, e.g. spine brass which is used for blocking the spine of a case prior to casing in. A true 'brass' is made by engraving the metal, brass, mechanically. The normally used brass is produced photomechanically on copper or zinc. See **chemac, zinco.**

brightness 1. Measure of a paper's reflectance of a standardized light. The result is expressed as an **ISO factor.** An 80gsm cartridge might be 85 ISO, for example. 2. Photographic term for the light reflected by the copy.

broadsheet Newspaper size approximating to A2 when folded.

bromide Photographic light-sensitive paper used in photographic reproduction or photo-typesetting, producing a positive image.

buckle folder Machine for sheet folding where the sheet is bent or buckled by a metal plate. Also called a **plate folder.** The main alternative folding method is knife folding on a **knife folder** (q.v.).

bulk Paper term used to describe the degree of thickness of paper. Measured by **caliper, volume or ppi pages per inch (American).**

bulky mechanical Grades of paper made predominantly from mechanical pulp to a specific and high bulk, e.g. as often used for cheap paperback books.

bullet Phototypesetting term for a large dot used for ornamentation.

bundling Compressing the folded sections at the beginning of the binding process. Carried out on a special bundling press or on an attachment to a sheet folder which squashes the sections flat and expels the air from them prior to further processing.

burst binding A form of unsewn adhesive binding where the sections are 'burst' or punched along the spines, thus giving extra adhesion between sheets as well as sections when the sections are bound. Also known as **punch binding.** See also **notch binding.**

C

calender A set of rollers on a paper machine which give a smooth finish to the web as it passes through by applying pressure. Calendered paper has a smooth, medium gloss finish. See also **supercalender.**

caliper The thickness of a sheet of paper or board, measured with a micrometer and usually expressed in thousandths-of-a-millimetre (microns).

camera ready artwork or camera ready copy (CRC) or camera ready paste-up (CRPU) Type-matter or type and line artwork pasted up into position ready for photographing.

Cameron belt press A web book press which, linked to a binding line, can print, gather and bind a book in one pass. Used primarily for paperbacks.

cap height The height of the capital letters of a fount.

caps Capitals. Upper-case letters, e.g. A, B, C, etc. See also **lower case.**

caption Text accompanying and describing an illustration.

caret Proof reader's mark indicating an insertion.

carrier sheet Sheet of paper inside film wrapping which carries the address label.

cartridge Printing or drawing paper with good dimensional stability, high opacity and good bulk. Often used in bookwork.

case 1. Stiff board cover of a book often covered with cloth, paper or leather which is attached to the **book-block** (q.v.) hence **case-bound. Casing-in** is the process of attaching the case to the book-block, often performed by a **casing-in machine.** 2. Partitioned tray containing metal or wooden type for hand composition. See also **lower case and upper case.**

case-bound Referring to a book with a hard case. Also cased. See also **limp-bound.**

casting off Calculating the number of pages a given amount of copy will make when set in a given type-face and size to a given area.

CCR Complementary colour removal. See **achromatic separation.**

centre To position type centrally in a given measure.

character compensation Global reduction or expansion in character fit by adjustment to the normal set width values resident in a typesetting system's computer. Also called **track kerning** or **tracking.**

character fit Space between letters which can be reduced or expanded.

character recognition Reading characters by machine, often for digital storage. Also, **optical character recognition, OCR.**

character set The full range of characters on a keyboard in memory or available for output from a machine.

chemical pulp Pulp obtained from wood or other plant sources by chemical removal of impurities rather than mechanical processing.

chemi-thermomechanical pulp CTMP Thermomechanical pulp (q.v.) which undergoes further chemical bleaching, resulting in a pulp not far below the quality of woodfree pulp. The very best quality of mechanical pulp made.

china clay White clay used for loading and coating paper.

cicero European 12pt unit of type measure. Equal to 4.511mm.

CIELab Scales of colour measurement used by the International Commission on Illumination.

close up Reduce spacing between characters of type or other elements on a proof.

coated cartridge Dull-finish coated paper, normally blade-coated, very commonly used for printing colour books.

coated paper Paper coated with china clay or similar to give a smooth surface suitable for half-tone reproduction.

code conversion The process of altering the numeric representation of one group of characters to that required by a different system or language.

cold colour Colour containing blue tones.

cold-set Web printing in which the ink is allowed

to dry by penetration on an absorbent paper without heat. See also heat-set.

collate Loosely used to mean **'gather'** (q.v.); but strictly, to check the gathered sections to establish that they are in the correct sequence. Collating marks on the back folds assist in this.

collating marks Black marks on the back folds of sections in sequential positions used for checking that the sections are in the correct order after gathering.

colophon A printer's or publisher's identifying symbol, printed on spines and title pages.

colour bars Coloured strips on four-colour pro–cess proofs showing densities across a sheet and revealing other printing characteristics.

colour-matching system Method of colour specification by matching the colour required to one in a swatch of colours provided as a set. Each colour in the swatch has its ink-mix formula described. An example is the **Pantone Matching System (PMS).**

colour separation Separating full colour into the four process colours by means of scanning or of filters, resulting in four films used to make printing plates.

combination folder A machine combining **buckle and knife units.**

complementary colour removal See **achromatic separations.**

compose To make up type into lines and/or pages. The operator is called a compositor.

composition sizes Types under 14pt in size. As distinct from **display sizes** (q.v.).

condensed type A typeface with narrow characteristics.

conditioning The deliberate exposure of paper to local atmospheric conditions so that its moisture content matches the ambient atmosphere.

contact print A photographic print of a negative or positive made in contact with, and therefore the same size as, the original.

contact screen Half-tone screen used in direct contact with the photographic film for creating half-tones.

continuous stationery Reel stationery used on computer printers and other automatic machines.

continuous tone Unscreened films containing genuine grey levels.

convertible press A press that will print on both sides of the sheet in one pass.

converting Sheeting, re-reeling or changing the format of sheets or reels of paper. The person who carries this out is known as a **converter.**

copyfitting Determining the typographical specification to which a manuscript needs to be set in order to fill a given amount of space.

copy prep Copy preparation. Putting instructions on a manuscript to ensure understanding of the requirement by the compositor. See also **electronic mark-up.**

copyright page Title page verso of a book containing bibliographic information. Also known as **biblio page.**

CPU Central processing unit. The computing unit in an electronic system.

CRC See **camera ready copy.**

Cromalin A proprietary plastic-laminate system for proofing four-colour subjects without making machine plates. See **plastic proof.**

crop Cut off part of an illustration to give better effect or achieve better fit.

cross grain Used to denote that the grain of the paper in a book runs at right-angles to the spine, not parallel to it (which is preferable). Also used to refer to endpapers as book covering materials in which the grain is at right angles to the spine.

cross head A sub-heading ranged centrally over text. As distinct from a **boxed head** which is ranged left.

CTMP Chemi-thermomechanical pulp (q.v.).

cut-off The web press measure of length of sheet cut, determined by the plate cylinder circumference. Measured in inches or mm.

cyrillic alphabet The Russian alphabet.

D

damper Roller on a litho press which transfers moisture to the plate prior to inking. Hence **damping solution.**

density Measurement of the tonal value of a printed or photographic area. Density is the light-stopping, or light-absorbing, ability of an object.

descender The part of a character which descends below the **base line** or **x-height,** e.g. y and p.

Didot The European measure of type. Based on a point of 0.376mm (0.0148"). Abbreviated to **D.**

die stamping An **intaglio** (q.v.) printing process from a steel die giving a relief surface on the paper.

dimension marks Marks on camera copy indicating the area of a reduction or enlargement.

DIN Deutsche Industrie Norme. The German standards institute. DIN paper sizes, now renamed **ISO** (q.v.) have been adopted as the European standard. See also **A series.**

direct litho Litho press system which transfers the image direct from the printing plate without offsetting it to a blanket first.

discretionary hyphens Hyphenation points for words, either held in the hyphenation exception dictionary of typesetting system or introduced while keyboarding new text. They indicate where a word may be broken if it needs to be hyphenated at the end of a line. Discretionary hyphens will overrule any logical hyphenation program in use.

display face A typeface designed for display sizes rather than for **composition sizes** (q.v.).

display sizes Sizes of type larger than 14pt, i.e. used for display rather than text.

dot 1. The individual element from which a half-tone reproduction is made up. 2. Synonym for **pixel** (q.v.). Dots per inch – dpi – is the standard measure of resolution, expressed as dots or pixels, for laser image output systems.

dot gain The enlargement of the half-tone dot which occurs during the mechanical processes of printing.

dpi Dots per inch. A measurement of **resolution** (q.v.) associated with output devices using laser imaging techniques.

drilling Perforating a pile of sheets with holes for special binding methods, such as loose-leaf.

drop cap(s) Drop capital. A letter or letters at the beginning of a paragraph which extend beyond the depth of the rest of the text line.

dry transfer lettering Sheets of typographic characters which can be transferred on to paper by rubbing.

dummy Mock-up of a book or other piece of printing to indicate specifications.

E

EBCDIC Extended Binary Coded Decimal Information Code. The code used by IBM mainframe computers.

edition binding Conventional, production-line, casebound binding.

electrostatic printing A process involving the reflection of light from an original on to an electrically charged drum. Areas affected by the light lose their charge. 'Toner', retained by the charged areas, is fused to paper, thereby creating an image. Also, **xerography, xerographic printing.** Laser printers use this principle for output.

emulsion Photosensitive coating on film or plate. Hence, **emulsion side.**

en Half the width of an **em** (q.v.). The width of the average type character, so is used as the basic unit of measurement for casting off copy. Also character or keystroke, in the sense of ens per hour (= characters set in one hour) or ens of setting (= character count in a manuscript).

endpaper Strong paper used for securing the body of a book to its case.

erratum slip Slip of paper pasted into a book and containing list of author's post-press corrections.

expanded type Typeface with characters wider than the normal fount.

F

family A series of founts related to the basic text roman face.

f&g sheets Folded and gathered sheets of a book.

feeder The mechanism on a press which separates and lifts sheets into the printing position.

film make-up Positioning pieces of film ready for platemaking. Page make-up is used as the term for pages or assembly for full imposition.

film processor Machine which automatically develops, fixes, washes and dries exposed film.

filmsetting Creating type on film by means of a photosetting system.

filter Coloured gelatin or glass sheet placed over a lens to eliminate specific colours reaching the film. Used to separate colours for process printing.

finish The type of surface on a particular grade of paper, e.g. machine finished or supercalendered. Also, varnish or lamination on a cover or jacket.

finishing Bindery processes taking place after a job is printed and bringing it to its final form ready for despatch, i.e. folding, stitching, cutting, inserting, etc.

flat artwork Artwork which is drawn on a solid base.

flat back Bound with a flat back (as distinct from 'rounded'). Also, **squareback.**

flatbed A press with the printing surface flat rather than curved as on a rotary press.

flat plan Diagrammatic scheme of the pagination. Indicates available colour positions, so that colour illustrations can be positioned for printing in the most economical way.

float Centre a piece of artwork in an area which is too large for it.

flush cover A cover trimmed flush with the pages of the text of the book.

flush left/right Type aligned with either the left or right-hand margins.

flying paster Pasting mechanism which joins a new reel of paper to that currently running out on a web press without stopping the press.

foil 1. Carrier for planned films 2. In bookbinding, short for stamping foil: a plastic film coated with clear or coloured lacquer and a thin layer of condensed aluminium, which is used to block covers.

folio 1. Page number at the head or foot of a page of text. 2. Sheet of copy.

foot Bottom of a book or page.

fore-edge Outer edge of a book, opposite the binding edge.

foreword Introduction to a book, not written by the author. As distinct from a **preface** (q.v.).

formation The fibre distribution of a sheet of paper. The two extremes are described as 'wild' or 'even'.

former folder Type of web press folder which draws paper over a **kite** (q.v.) to make first fold. As distinct from a **ribbon folder** (q.v.).

forwarding Binding stages from after sewing until casing-in.

fount A complete set of sorts all of the same typeface and point size.

frontmatter Prelims of a book.

G

gatefold A page in a magazine or book which folds out to double its size.

gathering Collecting sheets or signatures of a printed job into the correct sequence for binding. See also **collate.**

generic coding Coding the structure of a document rather than its typographical constituents.

ghosting An unintended faint printed image caused by problematic ink conditions, normally **ink starvation** (q.v.).

gloss art Shiny artpaper as opposed to matt art or coated carriage which have a dull finish.

goldenrod paper Opaque orange paper on which film is assembled for platemaking.

grain direction Direction of fibres in a sheet of paper. **Long grain** describes fibres running parallel with the longest side of a sheet; **short grain** along the shortest side. See also **machine direction.**

grammage Weight of paper expressed as grams per square metre.

graphics Pictures and illustrations in printed work.

gravure printing Process in which recesses on a cylinder are filled with ink and the surplus removed with a blade. The paper contacts the cylinder and 'lifts' the ink from the recesses. Used for long-run magazines and catalogues.

grey levels Separate tones of grey reflecting back from a continuous-tone original. Grey levels are frequently defined in 256 steps from pure white to pure black, each step identified by a different 8-bit number. The grey-level value of each **pixel** (q.v.) of an original is sampled by an analyse scanner in scanning an original and allocated its grey level value as one of these 256 steps.

grey scale Strip of grey tones from white to black, used to measure tonal range against a standard.

gripper Device on a printing press for holding the sheet.

gsm or g/m² Grams per square metre: the measure of substance of paper or board.

guillotine Machine which cuts paper into sheets. Programmatic guillotines can perform a whole series of measured cuts which have been preset.

gutter Binding margin of a book.

H

half sheet work See **work and turn.**

half-size press Printing press designed for a maximum sheet approximately 710 x 1010 mm (28" x 40"), i.e. half the size of a quad sheet. See also **mini-web.**

half-tone Illustration created by dots of varying size, resulting in the appearance of 'continuous tone'. Therefore, **half-tone negative** and **half-tone positive.**

half-tone screen Cross-ruled film or glass plate used to create half-tone dots. Dot formations can be round elliptical, rectangular, or pincushion. It can also be produced electronically.

h&j Hyphenation and justification.

hanging indent Typesetting style in which the first line of a paragraph is set full out and the remainder are indented.

hanging punctuation Punctuation marks at the end of justified lines which are allowed to jut out very slightly in order to give a visually straight right-hand edge to a column or page.

head Top or top margin of a page.

headband Cotton or silk cord attached to the top of the back of a book. See also **tailband**.

hickey Spot on a printed sheet caused by dust, lint or ink imperfections. Particularly noticeable in solids, large type half-tones, tints, etc.

highlights Lightest tonal values in a half-tone representing tonal values of 0% - 30%.

hold Retain matter for subsequent use.

hollow 1. Space between the case and the back of the sewn sections in a hardbound book. 2. By extension, the material used for reinforcing the inside spine of a case.

hopper Station on a machine (especially in binding) where printed sections are stacked and dropped on to a conveyer belt.

I

imperfection Book with printing or binding faults.

imposition Arrangement of pages in a sequence which will read consecutively when the printed sheet is folded. Hence **imposition scheme.**

impression 1. Pressure of the plate in contact with paper or blanket at the moment of printing. 2. All the copies of a book from one printing.

imprint Publisher's and/or printer's identifying text printed in a book or other work.

inferior Small character set below the base line at the foot of another character.

initial First letter in text when set in such a way that it stands out, e.g. bigger than its normal cap text size.

ink jet printer A non-impact printing mechanism which forms the image by deflecting ink droplets electromagnetically.

intaglio Printing from a recessed image, e.g. gravure, die stamping, etc.

intermediates Films used in the intermediate stages of reproduction between the original and final printing films. Normally continuous tone.

International Organization for Standardization (ISO) The organisation which co-ordinates the drawing-up of internationally accepted standards.

iph Impressions per hour. A measure of printing speed.

ISO sizes Formerly **DIN sizes** (q.v.). International range of paper and envelope sizes, comprising **A series, B series, and C series.**

italic Specially designed letters that slope forward. Contrast **sloped roman.**

J

jacket Dust cover on book.

jog Align edges of a pile of papers by vibrating them.

justification The spacing of words to a predetermined measure, giving 'straight' left and right margins.

K

kern Part of a typographic character projecting beyond the body.

kerning Adjusting the amount of space to improve the uniformity and appearance of a word or line.

keyline Line on artwork which indicates an area for tint-laying, positioning of half-tones etc., or any other area where work must be done at reproduction stage.

knife folder A type of folding machine which uses a knife between inwardly rotating rollers. Contrast **buckle folder** (q.v.).

knocking up To line up the edges of a pile of paper.

L

lamination Thin plastic film applied by heat and pressure to a printed sheet for protection and/or appearance. See also **OPP lamination.**

landscape Page format size, or illustration, that is wider than it is deep. As distinct from **portrait.**

lap Extent by which one side of a folded section overlaps the other. Often necessary for automatic binding machines.

lay Guide on a printing machine which positions a sheet before printing.

lay down Impose a job.

leading The spacing between lines of type. Also **interlinespacing, film advance, film feed.**

leading edge The edge of a sheet or plate at which printing begins.

leaf Single sheet, comprising two pages.

letter-fit Spacing between characters in a typeface.

letterset Also called dry offset, offset letterpress, and indirect letterpress. A relief plate transfers the image to a blanket and thence on to the paper.

letterspacing The introduction of small amounts of space between letters to aid with justification. Typographically undesirable except with capitals, which often benefit from a small amount of letterspacing.

light primaries See **additive primaries.**

light secondaries The complementary, or 'opposite' colours to the additive primaries.

lightweight paper Normally taken to mean paper less than 60g/m·in substance.

limp binding Paperback binding.

lining figures Arabic numerals the same height as capitals, also known as **aligning numerals.** As distinct from **non-lining or old-style figures** (q.v.).

literal Mistake introduced in keyboarding, often only affecting one or two characters.

litho See **lithography.**

lithography Planographic process in which ink is applied selectively to the plate by chemically treating the image areas to accept ink and the non-image areas to accept water. Shortened to **litho.**

logo See **logotype.**

logotype Company name or product device used in a special design as a trademark. Shortened to **logo.**

long grain Sheet of paper in which the grain direction (or machine direction) runs parallel with the longest side.

long ton Imperial ton (2240lb), equal to 1.12 short (US) tons, or 1.0161 metric tonnes.

lower case Small letters as distinct from capitals. Abbreviated as **lc.**

M

M 1. Abbreviation for 1000. 2. Used to indicate the machine direction (grain direction) of a sheet when placed against one dimension, e.g. 890(M) x 1130 is a **short grain** sheet (q.v.).

machine coated Paper coated on the paper-making machine.

machine direction The direction in which fibres lay on the wire of a paper machine, i.e. along the web. Also called grain direction. As distinct from the cross direction (q.v.).

machine finished (MF) Smooth paper calendered on the paper machine.

machining Printing.

macro A sequence of characters, possibly defined and stored by the user, which may be accessed by the depression of a single key.

magenta Process red. One of the colours used in four-colour process printing.

magnetic ink character recognition The ability of suitable devices to identify characters printed in magnetic ink.

make-ready Setting up a printing machine ready to run a specific job.

make-up Making-up typeset material into pages.

making order An order for paper to particular specifications needing to be made specially rather than withdrawn from stock.

making-up Assembly of printed sections prior to sewing.

mask Opaque overlay which masks out the unwanted portion of a photograph.

Matchprint Proprietary plastic laminated proof, similar to a Cromalin.

measure Length of line of type.

mechanical paper Paper made from **mechanical pulp** (q.v.).

mechanical pulp Pulp produced mechanically, by grinding, rather than chemically. There are several sorts.

metallic inks Inks containing metallic powders to give a gold or silver printed effect. Best printed in conjunction with a **primer** (q.v.).

mid tones or middle tones Tonal ranges between highlights and shadows.

mini-web Small web offset machine typically producing 16pp A4 colour sections (8p A4 to view). Also known as **narrow-web,** or **half-size press.**

10

misprint Typographical error.

misregister One colour or more printed out of alignment with other colours.

moiré Undesirable pattern caused by incorrect angles of screens.

N

narrow web See **mini-web.**

negative assembly Combining negatives on a flat ready for platemaking.

negative-positive print The standard colour 'n' print.

negative-working plates Litho plates which are exposed using negatives.

newsprint Paper made from mechanical pulp for the printing of newspapers, usually between 45 and 58gsm.

non-lining figures See **old-style figures.**

notch binding A form of unsewn binding in which notches are punched in the backs of the sections as they are folded on the folding machine, and glue applied in through the notches to hold the leaves together. Also called **slotted binding.** See also **burst binding.**

O

OCR Optical Character Recognition. The interpretation of typewritten or printed characters by a machine which scans the text and stores it in memory, possibly for subsequent typesetting.

octavo Abbreviated as 8vo. The eighth part of the traditional broadside sheet. Used to describe book sizes, e.g. Demy Octavo.

oddment A book signature with fewer pages than the others and which has to be printed separately.

offprint Part of a book or journal printed separately, e.g. an article from a journal.

offset Printing which uses an intermediate medium to transfer the image on to paper, e.g. a rubber blanket wrapped around a cylinder as in **offset litho.**

old-style figures Also called **non-lining figures.** Numerals which do not align on the base line but have ascenders and descenders. As distinct from **modern** or **lining figures.**

on the fly Refers to any process which occurs as digital data is being transferred, such as the screening of half-tones simultaneously with output to an image recorder.

opacity The quality of opaqueness in a paper. Opacity is measured in %, with around 90% being an average for 80g/m² printing paper.

opaque 1. To paint out areas on film with an opaque paint. 2. The paint used in opaquing, also called **photopaque.**

optical brightener Dye which emits visible radiation. Used to 'brighten' paper.

optical centre The 'visual' centre of a page, about 10% higher than the mathematical centre.

optical character recognition See **OCR.**

origination All the processes involved in the reproduction of original material, including make-up, up to plate-making stages; and also including typesetting.

orphan The first line of a new paragraph, or a subhead, which appears at the foot of a page. Considered undesirable. See also **widow, clubline.**

out-turn sheet Sheet of paper taken during manufacture or on delivery as a representative sample for checking specification.

overlay 1. Transparent cover to artwork containing instructions or additional detail. 2. Paper used on machine cylinder to increase pressure on solid areas of blocks.

overmatter Typeset matter which was not used in the final printing.

ozalid Print made by a form of diazo copying process and often used for proofing film. See also **blueprint.**

P

page One side of a leaf.

page description language PDL In desktop publishing, software necessary for the composition of combined text and graphics, encompassing factors such as scaling, font rotation, graphics and angles. Some examples, such as Adobe's PostScript, are device-independent. Other PDLs include Interpress from Xerox, PCL from Hewlett-Packard and Interleaf's RIP print.

panchromatic film Photographic material sensitive to all colours.

Pantone Proprietary name of a widely used colour-matching system.

part-mechanical paper Paper containing up to 50% of mechanical pulp with the balance chemical pulp. Compare **mechanical paper, woodfree paper.**

PDL See **page description language.**

pel See **pixel.**

perfect binding Adhesive binding widely used on paperbacks and magazines. Glue is applied to the roughened back edges of sections to hold them to the cover and each other. Also called **adhesive binding, cut-back binding, thermoplastic binding, threadless binding.**

perfecting Printing both sides of a sheet at one pass. Such a press is called a **perfector.**

permanent paper Paper which is acid-free and made to stringent conditions for archival purposes. The accepted standard for manufacture is laid out in American standard ANSI Z39 1984 and specifies neutral pH, alkaline reserve, chemical furnish, and specified tear resistance and fold endurance.

photomechanical transfer Abbreviated to PMT. Paper negative which produces a positive print by a process of chemical transfer. Used for line artwork and screened prints.

photopolymer plate Letterpress flexographic printing plate made with **photopolymer** material.

pica 1. Unit of typographic measurement equal to 12 points or 4.218mm (0.166044"). 2. Size of typewriter face with 10 characters to the inch.

pi characters Special characters outside the normal alphabetic range and not normally contained in a standard fount, e.g. special maths symbols.

picture element See **pixel.**

pin register system The use of holes and pins to provide a system of aligning copy, film and plates in register. The Protocol system is one of the best known. Also **punch register system.**

pixel From PICture ELements; the minute individual image/non-image areas created by the digitization of type or graphics. A pixel is the smallest element of a displayed image that can be addressed. Also **pel.**

planning All the processes involved in imposition, laying pages down on to foils in imposition sequence, etc, ready for platemaking.

planographic printing Printing from a flat (as distinct from indented or relief) image, e.g. litho.

plastic proof Proof such as Cromalin, Matchprint, etc. made by exposing colour separations to a special material which images in the process colours corresponding to each separation. Also called a **pre-press proof.** As distinct from a **machine proof** (wet proof) which is made by printing from plates.

PMS Pantone Matching System. See **Pantone.**

PMT See **photomechanical transfer.**

point system The main system of typographic measurement. 1pt =0.351mm (0.013837"). See also **didot, pica.**

portrait The shape of an image or page with the shorter dimension at the head and foot, as distinct from landscape.

positive An image on film or paper in which the dark and light values are the same as the original, as distinct from **negative**.

PostScript Adobe System's page description language. Achieved prominence through its adoption by Apple, and currently the most widely used **PDL**.

primary (subtractive) colours Yellow, magenta, and cyan which, with black, make up the four **process colours.**

printer's error See **PE.**

printing down Laying film over a light-sensitive plate or paper to produce an image.

print to paper Instruction to the printer to use all available paper for a job, rather than printing to a specific quantity of copies.

progressive proofs or progs Proofs of each plate in a colour set showing each colour alone and in combination with the others as a guide to colour matching, at the printing stage.

projection platemaking equipment Equipment such as the Rachwal system which makes plates by exposing from 35mm or 70mm roll micro-films mounted in the head of computer-controlled step-and-repeat machines. The microfilm contains the pages of the job shot sequentially; the step-and-project machine is programmed to locate and expose each page in imposition order on to the plate.

punch register system Device which punches registered holes in sets of films or plates for positioning puposes. Also, **pin register system.**

Q

quad 1. Paper terminology for a sheet four times the size of the traditional broadside sheet, e.g. 'Quad Demy', 890 x 1130 mm. 2. Letterpress spacing material used to fill out lines of type.

quarto A page one-quarter of the traditional broadside sheet size, e.g. Crown Quarto.

R

range Align (type, etc.).

raster image processor (RIP) Device which links the page assembly workstation and the imagesetter interpreting the data and converting it into raster format as well as screening halftones and separating colours.

ream Five hundred sheets of paper.

recto A right-hand page.

reflection copy Copy viewed by its reflected light, e.g. a photograph, as distinct from **transmission copy** (q.v.), which is viewed by transmitted light.

register 1. Positioning of colours accurately to form a composite image.

repro Pre-press camerawork, scanning and film make-up. Also, **origination.**

reproduction See **repro.**

resolution Measurement of image fineness stated in lines per inch (**lpi**), dots per inch (**dpi**), or **pixels** per inch as created by an output device such as a scanner, imagesetter, laser typesetter, or laser printer.

revise A revised proof for subsequent reading.

ribbon folder Web press folder which cuts web into ribbons for folding. As distinct from a **former folder** (q.v.).

right-reading Film which reads 'correctly', i.e. from left to right, when viewed from the emulsion side. As distinct from **wrong-reading** (q.v.).

roman figures Roman numerals such as iii, xviii, xxv, etc.

roman type 'Upright' letters as distinct from **italic** (q.v.). Known as **plain** or **normal** in DTP systems.

rounding and backing Also **rounding and jointing.** Shaping a book so the back is convex. As distinct from **flat back binding.**

running head A title repeated at the top of each page. Also known as **running headline.**

S

saddle-stitching Binding magazines and inset books with wire staples through the middle fold of sheets. Also, **saddle wire-stitching.**

sans serif A typeface with no **serifs** (q.v.).

screen 1. Pattern of lines that creates the dot formation in half-tones (q.v.) As well as the normal crossline screen at 45°, other screens include the vertical screen at 90°, one-way screen, linen screen, textured screen, mezzotint screen, etc.

screen angles Varied angles of each screen used in colour half-tones to avoid moiré patterns. The conventional screen angles are:

black	45^0
magenta	75^0
yellow	90^0
cyan	$105^0(15^0)$

screen process printing See **silk screen printing.**

screen ruling The number of lines or dots per inch on a screen. The conventional screen rulings in common use for bookwork are 100, 120, 133, 150 lines per inch (40, 48, 54, 60 lines per centimetre).

section A folded sheet forming part of a book.

separation See **colour separation, origination.**

separation negative See **colour separation negative.**

series A complete range of sizes in the same typeface.

serifs The short cross lines on the ends of ascenders, descenders and strokes of letters in certain typefaces.

set-off The transfer of wet ink to another sheet. Typically occurs at the delivery end of the printing press. Precautions can include the use of an anti-setoff spray.

sheetwise Printing one side of a sheet at a time. As distinct from **perfecting** (q.v.).

sheetwork To print each side of the sheet from a separate forme. Each sheet yields one copy. As distinct from **work and turn** (q.v.).

short-grain Sheet of paper in which the grain is parallel to the short edge of the sheet.

show-through Lack of opacity in a sheet of paper to the point where the printed image on one side of a page is excessively visible from the reverse side.

side-stabbing Used loosely to describe side **wire-stitching** (q.v.). But strictly, a form of stitching where the stitch on one side of the book penetrates only two-thirds distance, and a complementary stitch at the other side completes the securing.

signature 1. The letters of the alphabet or numerals printed at the bottom left-hand corner of sections to show the correct sequence of sections. 2. Synonym for **section** (q.v.).

silk screen printing Method which employs a fine mesh to support a stencil through which ink is squeezed.

small capitals or small caps Abbreviated sc. Capitals the same size as the x-height of the normal lower case. As distinct from full **capitals** (q.v.).

soft hyphen A hyphen introduced into a word by an H&J program, as opposed to a hard **hyphen** grammatically essential to the word.

solid 1. Typeset with no leading between the lines. 2. Printed area with 100 per cent ink coverage.

sort 1. A single character of type. 2. To order data into a given sequence, e.g. alphabetical.

spot colour Single additional second colour printed in a black working.

s/s Abbreviation for 'same size' in reproduction specifications.

subscript Inferior character. Small character printed below the base line as part of mathematic equation.

substance Paper weight measured in grams per square metre.

subtractive primaries Yellow, magenta and cyan, the process colours.

supercalender A calendering stack with alternate hard steel rollers and soft rollers which imparts a high gloss finish to paper as it 'slips' between them. Usually off-machine.

superior Small character set above the line especially used in mathematical statements (e.g. 106) or to indicate footnotes.

swatch Colour specimen printed on paper or a set of such specimens.

T

tag A generic mark-up tag is one which identifies a particular atttribute: an 'A' heading, for example, in the mark-up of text. Tags are converted to typesetting by allocating typographical specifications to them and translating them in the typesetting system.

tails Bottom margins of pages.

text type Body type of the main text in a book. Loosely, a composition size of type of 14pt or less, as opposed to a **display type.**

thermographic printing Relief effect created by heating special powder or ink on a sheet to give 'raised' typesetting.

thermomechanical pulp Abbreviated to **TMP.** Superior, stronger **mechanical pulp** (q.v.) produced from steam-heated wood chips.

thread sewing Conventional book sewing. Also known as **French sewing** or **section sewing.**

tint A solid colour reduced in shade by screening. Specified as a percentage of the solid colour, and in a particular **screen ruling** (q.v.).

tip in To fix a single leaf inside a section.

tip on To fix a single leaf, or endpaper, to the outside of a section.

tonne Metric tonne, equivalent to .984 long (imperial) tons, or 1.102 short (US) tons.

to view Referring to the number of pages appearing on one side of a plate or sheet, e.g. 32-to-view = 32pp each side of the sheet = 64pp unit.

transfer type Pressure-sensitive type on carrier sheets. Can be rubbed off to create type in position on the page. Also known as **transfer lettering.**

transmission copy Copy which is viewed by transmitted light, e.g. a transparency. As distinct from **reflection copy** (q.v.) which is viewed by reflected light.

transparency Full-colour photographic positive on transparent film for viewing by transmitted light. Suitable as copy for separation.

transparent copy or "see" Transparencies (q.v.).

transpose Abbreviated **trs.** Exchange the position of words, letters or lines, especially on a proof. Hence **transposition.**

trap Superimposition of one colour on another when printing. Trapping characteristics are often monitored by a test strip in the colour bars printed on a four-colour job.

trim marks Alternative term for **crop marks** (q.v.) or **tick marks.**

type series All the sizes available in one typeface.

typographer Designer of printed material.

typographic errors Abbreviated to typos. See **literals.**

U

U/L or ulc Upper and lower case.

unbacked Printed one side only.

uncoated paper Paper with no coating and therefore not suitable for high quality illustrated work.

undercolour removal Abbreviated to UCR. Technique which reduces unwanted colour in areas of overlaps. Results in better trapping and lower ink cost.

unjustified Typesetting with even spacing, therefore having a ragged right edge.

unsewn binding See **perfect binding.**

upper case Capital letters.

UV varnish Ultra-violet varnish. Can be installed in-line with a printing machine, a UV varnish unit deposits a high-gloss varnish dried by exposure to UV light.

V

vacuum frame Contact printing frame using vacuum pumps to hold copy down in position.

value Lightness or darkness of tone.

varnish Thin, transparent coating applied to printed work for gloss or protection.

verso Left-hand page with even number.

volume 1. Bound book. 2. Thickness of paper expressed as a volume number (e.g. vol 18) equal to the thickness in millimetres of 100 sheets of paper in 100gsm.

W

warm colours Red and yellow shades.

web A continuous length of paper (i.e. a roll or reel) as distinct from sheets.

web offset Reel-fed offset litho.

wet-on-wet Superimposition of colours on a multi-unit press (i.e. before each colour has dried).

widow Short last line of a paragraph at the top of a page. Considered undesirable. See also **paragraph widow, orphan.**

wipe-on-plate Litho plate to which the light-sensitive coating is applied by hand or by whirler.

with the grain In the direction of the length of the original web. Paper folds more easily with the grain.

woodfree pulp Pulp which is processed chemically and which contains no mechanical groundwood.

word break Division of a word at a line ending.

work and tumble Printing the reverse side of a sheet by turning it over on its long axis from gripper to back and using the same plate. Each sheet, cut in half, yields two copies.

work and turn Printing the first side of a sheet, turning the stack across its short axis, and then printing the reverse side of the sheet using the same plate and the same gripper edge. Each sheet, cut in half, yields two copies.

workings Number of passes through a printing machine to make up a complete job, e.g. four workings on a single-colour press to produce a four-colour print or one working on a four-colour press.

wrong-reading Film which reads incorrectly, i.e. reversed from left to right, when viewed from the emulsion side. Also called **reverse-reading.**

X,Y,Z

xenon flash Intense momentary light source used in photosetting.

xerography Electrostatic copying process in which toner adheres to charged paper to produce an image.

x-height Height of body of lower-case letters, exclusive of ascenders and descenders, i.e. height of the letter x.

x-line Alignment along the tops of lower-case letters. Also, **mean line** (q.v.).

yankee dryer Steam-heated paper drying cylinder generating a glazed finish.

yapp cover Binding material edges which overlap the case boards to provide a 'fringed' effect. Often used on Bibles.

zinc engraving Relief engraving made on zinc and often used for short-run blocking in preference to a chemac. Also called **zinco.**

Zip-a-tone Proprietary name for patterned line or dot effects applied as rub-down film on to artwork. See also **Letraset, transfer type.**

Index

Index

Index

Index

Main text 16, 20-4
  display heads 23
  running heads 27
  subheads 23
Make-up
  film 133-5
  manual 133
  materials 131-3
  paper 133, 135-7
Manilla paper 185
Manuscript 15
  additional matter 15-16
  assembly 15-16
  bookwork 16
  camera-ready copy 16
  magazine work 16
Margins 15
  proportion 21
  text setting 21-2
Marina 12
Mark-up 18-29
  areas of responsibility 18
  illustrations 24-6
  printing considerations 28-9
  typographical considerations 20-4
Masking strip film 140
Matchprint (3Ms) 135
Mathematical setting for keyboards 69
Mathematical symbols 17, 39-40
Matt coated paper 184, 189
McCain sewing 215
Measurement systems 6-9
  Anglo-American 6, 233
  European 6, 233
  metric typographic 1
Measures
  conversion 231-2
  Imperial 230
  metric 229
Mechanical binding 215-16
Mechanical papers 183-4
Media conversion 49, 51
  complications 53
Media converters 51
Medium 3
Melior 13
Metallic ink 211

Metric multiples 231
Metric typographic measurement 1
Metric-Imperial conversion 232
Microelite 65
Microsoft Word 74
Millboard 224
Mistral 12
Modem 52
Modern Extended 11
Modern typeface *see* Didone typeface
Modular unit machines 152-3
  four colour 153
Moffat sewing 215
Moire 63
Monochrome reproduction 104-11
  line reproduction 104-6
  tone reproduction 105-9
Mottle 189-90
Multi-colour images, die stamping
  180, 181
Multi-colour litho printing
  half-tones 166-7
  quality control 166-9, 168
  textmatter 166
Multi-colour machines 152-3
  converter 153
  in-line 152
  letterpress second printing unit 154
  modular unit 152-3
  second printing designs 154
  small-offset 154
Multi-colour planning 140-1
  blue keys 141
  pin register 140-1
  positive film elements 140
  red keys 141
Multi-colour printing
  positive-working plate 144
  ribbon folder 163
Multi-colour thermography 181-2
Multi-metal plate
  chrome addition 149
  negative-working multi-steel 148-9
  positive-working 149
  surface-working presensitized 148

Index

Tables
  batch pagination 88
  presentational style 17
  text setting conventions 21
Tagged Image File Format (TIFF) 102-3
Tail 142
Tail end hook 191
Tandem machines *see* In-line machines
Telecommunications 49, 52-3
Telephone line digital data transmission 52
Telescoped reel 191-2
Temperature control for waterless plate 148
Text
  factual accuracy 18
  galley make-up 131
  input 68-75
  manipulation software 73
  preparation 15
  reformatting 48
  setting 21-2
  transfer 50
Textile printing 177
Textual notes 27-8
Thermal dye sublimation printers 126
Thermography 181-2
  multi-colour 181-2
Thermoplastic coating 147, 148
Thermosetting powder 181
Third generation film 104, 106
Thread-sealing 220, 222
Thread-sewing 215-16
Three-knife trimmer 157, 221
  in-line 204, 212
Thumb indexing 204
Tilde 41
Times 21
Tints 134
Tipping-in 202-3
Tissues 183
Title page 20
Titles, italic 19
Tone originals
  black and white 96-7
  colour 97-9
Tone reproduction 105-9

duotone reproduction 108-9
half-tone
  on diffusion transfer material 107
  from printed copy 108
  negatives 106
  screen formation 105-6
  screenless reproduction 109
Toner 170-1
  dry 124
Transitional typeface 11
Transmission copy 95, 97-8, 99, 100
Trapping 125
  patches 129
Treble-column setting 22
Trimming 157, 204, 212
Turner bars 161
Two-shot binding 214
Type
  area
    exclusive 22, 55
    inclusive 22
    text setting 21-2
  family 2-3
  measure 21, 232-3
  point size 21, 233
  series 3
  size
    column setting 22
    multi-colour litho printing 166
  weight 3
  width 3
  see also Fount
Type-and-tone effect 96
Typeface
  choice 21
  classification 10-13
  coded in word processing programs 73
  colour use 28
  design 10-13
  digital information 60-1
  hairline serif 28, 96, 165
  humanist 10-11
  multi-colour litho printing 166
  proportions 10
  reproduction on laser printers 77
  serif formation 10
  set width 56